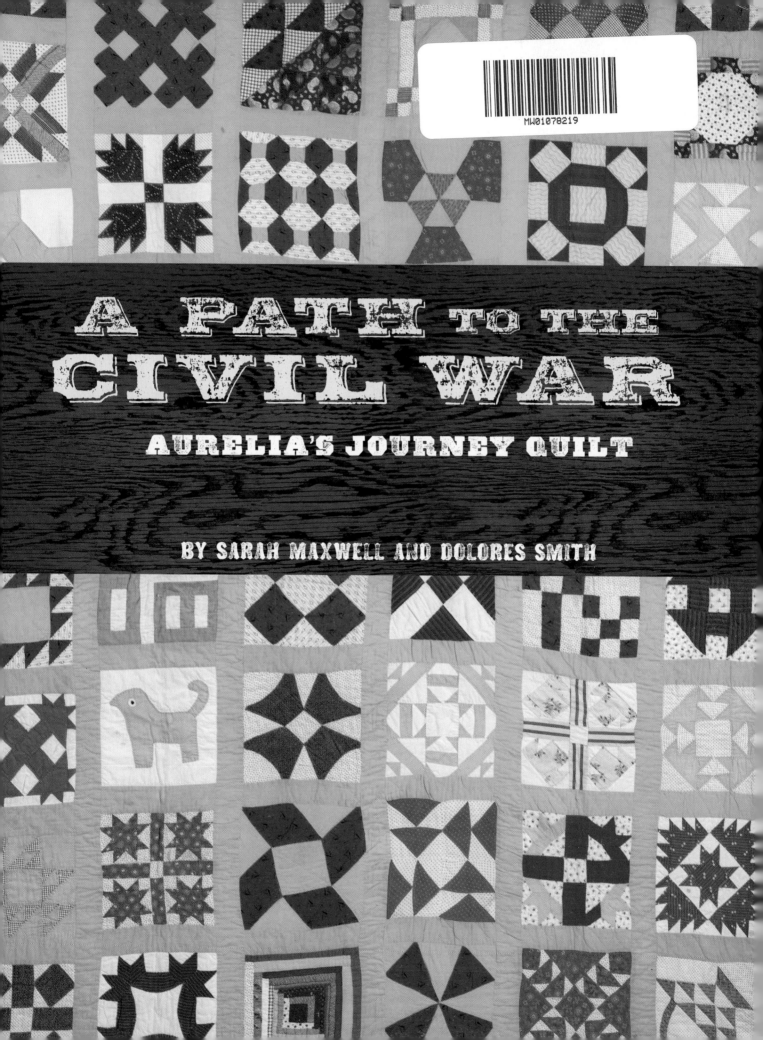

A PATH TO THE CIVIL WAR

AURELIA'S JOURNEY QUILT

BY SARAH MAXWELL AND DOLORES SMITH

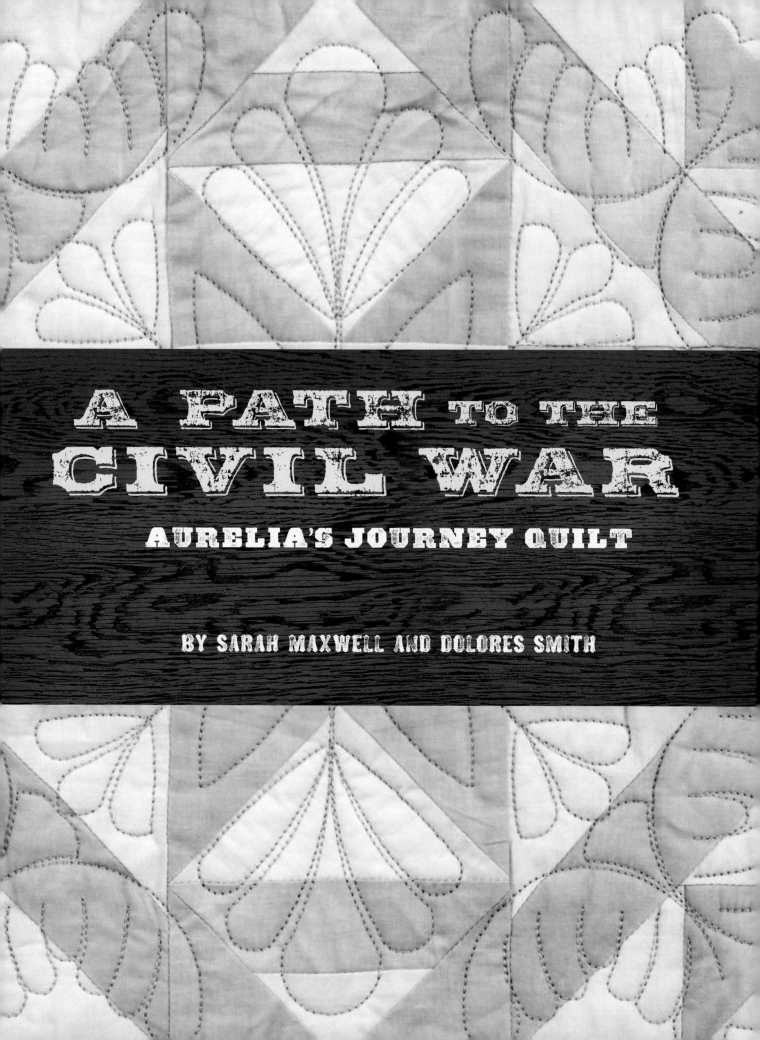

A PATH TO THE CIVIL WAR

AURELIA'S JOURNEY QUILT

BY SARAH MAXWELL AND DOLORES SMITH

DEDICATION

This book is dedicated to all the quilters throughout time who have turned to their craft in times of conflict and difficulty. Only those of us in the community of quilters understand how comforting the cutting, piecing and processes of quilting can be.

ACKNOWLEDGEMENTS

Developing the history and patterns for Aurelia's Journey has been a labor of love. Of course, any project like this takes time which means time not spent with our families. So, first and foremost, from Sarah to my husband Joe and daughters Megan & Shannen and from Dolores to my husband Brian and son, Kyle and my angels above that look over us, Ryan and Breigha, thank you for all you do to support our quilting and for your continued support and love.

To our girls (who are grown women) at the shop that put up with our craziness and our many projects.

To the fantastic team at the Kansas City Star, especially Doug Weaver and Diane McLendon, we appreciate you embracing our concept and publishing this book.

To our patient editor, Jenifer Dick, thanks for putting up with our busy schedules and offering your insight and expertise. We would also like to thank our designer, Brian Grubb and photographer, Aaron Leimkuehler.

Thanks to Marcus Fabrics, especially Pati Violick for working with us to develop a fabric line for this project, to Faye Burgos for helping us come up with the perfect cheddar and to Stephanie Dell'Olio for keeping fabric in production so quilters can recreate this project.

We hope you enjoy joining Aurelia on her journey as you make your own sampler quilt.

A PATH TO THE CIVIL WAR
BY SARAH MAXWELL AND DOLORES SMITH

EDITOR
JENIFER DICK

DESIGNER
BRIAN GRUBB

PHOTOGRAPHY
AARON T. LEIMKUEHLER

ILLUSTRATION
LON ERIC CRAVEN

TECHNICAL EDITOR
NAN DOLJAC

PRODUCTION ASSISTANCE
JO ANN GROVES

Published by:
Kansas City Star Books
1729 Grand Blvd.
Kansas City, Missouri, USA 64108

All rights reserved
Copyright © 2010
The Kansas City Star Co.

First edition, first printing
ISBN: 978-1-935362-50-0

Library of Congress Control Number:
2010931578

Printed in the United States of America by
Walsworth Publishing Co., Marceline, MO

To order copies, call StarInfo at
(816) 234-4636 and say "Books."

KANSAS CITY STAR QUILTS
Continuing the Tradition

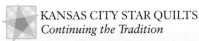
The Quilter's Home Page

CONTENTS

A PATH TO WAR

A PATH TO WAR

As our nation nears the 150th anniversary of the start of the Civil War, people of all ages remain fascinated by this period of history. Whether it be commemorative battlefields and tour sites, re-enactments or fabrics typical of the era, almost everyone can find some aspect of the war that catches their interest.

The war, which officially began April 12, 1861, with the first shots fired at Fort Sumter, South Carolina, seems inextricably linked to the conflict over slavery. However, many issues across the nation fueled the tensions that ultimately led to the war between the states. George Santayana famously said "Those who cannot learn from history are doomed to repeat it." In school, history was always my least favorite topic. Hearing about people and events from long ago seemed so boring and pointless. Now, as an adult, I appreciate learning about events that shaped our nation.

A NATION DIVIDED

While the question of slavery prompted much of the discord in our nation during the 1800s, other social and political issues also led the country to war. Economic differences between the North and South, the geographical expansion of the United States and a lack of understanding among various factions in the developing country all played a part.

As these historic events unfolded across the United States, did women turn to quilting as a way to relieve stress and take their minds off troubling topics? When Dolores and I found this antique sampler quilt completed June 2, 1875, by Aurelia (pronounced oar-LEE-uh) Bevins of Broome, New York, we wondered if the maker worked on the quilt as a diversion from the issues of the day. This sampler quilt was undoubtedly pieced over a long period of time. Stitched by hand, the top includes a large number of varied fabrics suggesting the quilter collected materials for the project over a long period.

The cheddar fabric used as the sashing, borders and in some blocks was very popular in the 1830s-1860s while other fabrics are more typical of the mid-late 1800s. Completed after the Civil War, it's easy to imagine that Aurelia worked on this project off and on for many years as she witnessed a country at war with itself.

AURELIA'S JOURNEY

The variety of blocks is intriguing ranging from the simple Shoo Fly to complex, intricate blocks with many small pieces. The bright, cheddar sashing so typical of mid-1800s quilts brings these diverse blocks together.

Of course, like many quilters of the era, Aurelia was not overly concerned with matching seams or whether her blocks fit into their allotted size in the quilt. To make things easier for today's quilters, we redrafted the blocks. In the original quilt, blocks in the two outer rows are approximately 9″ finished while blocks in the inner rows range from 10″ to 11″ finished. The maker forced these varying sized blocks into their assigned spot in the quilt resulting in chopped-off points and wobbly rows. To make our piecing more precise while retaining the original's charm, we opted for making blocks in the two outermost rows at 9″ finished while blocks in the interior of the quilt are 12″ finished.

As you read about the causes of the Civil War and stitch your own sampler, think of Aurelia and her journey. Did she work in the evening as she listened to her husband and other relatives discuss the news of the day? Did she have a family member in the military who fought in one of the great battles of the Civil War? Was this quilt a way to occupy her time while she waited on someone to come home? Use this quilt to calm your own nerves over whatever stresses are in your life.

- Sarah Maxwell

CHOOSING FABRICS FOR YOUR JOURNEY

As you recreate Aurelia's Journey, you may use your own fabrics and colors or you may choose to recreate it exactly as shown in the following patterns. Marcus Fabrics has produced a cheddar yellow print that we used in the sashing. We also selected a variety of current Marcus Fabrics prints for the blocks. A downloadable flyer with the fabric numbers is available at our website, **www.homesteadhearth.com** if you want to recreate the quilt as shown. Fabrics are available on our website or from your local quilt shop.

AURELIA'S JOURNEY

SIZE: 88 1/2″ X 107″ • BLOCKS: 9″ FINISHED AND 12″ FINISHED SQUARE

MADE BY: DOLORES SMITH AND SARAH MAXWELL

QUILTED BY: CONNIE GRESHAM

FABRIC REQUIREMENTS

FOR THE BLOCKS

4 yards of assorted light background prints and solids ranging in color from aged muslin to tan
1/2 yard of assorted black prints
2 1/4 yards of assorted brown prints
1 1/2 yards of assorted red prints
3/4 yard of assorted pink prints
1 1/3 yard of assorted blue prints
1/4 yard of green print

FOR THE SASHING AND BORDERS

6 yards of cheddar

Using the instructions starting on page 14, make 44 blocks. Two blocks are repeated and noted in the patterns. Once the blocks are made, arrange them in the desired order.

PUTTING IT ALL TOGETHER

Aurelia's Journey is set in rows with the two outer rows composed of 9″ finished blocks and the center 4 rows composed of 12″ finished blocks. Sashing separates the blocks in the rows and long strips separate the rows. See assembly diagram on page 11.

BLOCK SASHING

From the cheddar, cut
OUTER ROWS
14 – 3 1/4″ x 9 1/2″ strips.
4 – 5 7/8″ x 9 1/2″ strips.
INNER ROWS
24 – 3 1/2″ x 12 ½″ strips.

ASSEMBLY

OUTER ROWS
Sew a 3 1/4″ sashing strip in between the 8 blocks. Press to the sashing. Sew the two 5 7/8″ strips to the top and bottom. Press to the sashing. Repeat with the opposite outer row.

INNER ROWS
Sew a 3 1/2″ sashing strip in between the 7 blocks. Press to the sashing.

ROW SASHING
From the cheddar, cut:
13 strips 4″ x width of fabric.

Piece the strips together to make 5 strips measuring 4″ x 102 1/2″. Sew the strips in between the center 4 rows. Press to the sashing. Sew the outer rows to the center rows, creating the top center.

BORDERS

OUTER BORDERS
From the cheddar, cut: 6 – 3″ strips.

TOP AND BOTTOM BORDERS
From the cheddar, cut: 5 – 3″ strips.

ASSEMBLY

OUTER BORDER
Piece the strips together to make 2 strips measuring 3″ x 102 ½″. Sew these borders to opposite sides of the quilt. Press to the borders.

TOP AND BOTTOM BORDERS
Piece the strips together to make 2 strips measuring 3″ x 89″. Sew these borders to top and bottom of the quilt. Press to the borders.

BINDING

FROM THE CHEDDAR, CUT:
11 – 2 1/2″ x width of fabric strips.

Piece strips together to create about 450″ of binding. Fold in half lengthwise, press and attach to quilt after quilting as desired.

GENERAL INSTRUCTIONS

The blocks in this book are constructed with a variety of methods including rotary cutting, machine piecing, and machine appliqué. In these instructions, we will share our favorite methods and tips. Of course, feel free to adapt anything to the methods you prefer. We firmly believe that the best quilt is a finished quilt. And, we love antique and primitive quilts so we seldom worry about perfectly lining up stripes or rotating every single piece so the fabric is perfectly oriented. At the same time, we value sharp points and accurately-sized blocks. These tips should aid in achieving those goals.

FABRIC

Quality of fabric makes a difference in the finished result! Your local quilt shop will generally sell top-quality, 100% cotton fabrics suitable for piecing and quilting. If you're going to take time to make a quilt, why not invest in the best materials possible so your work lasts?

PRE-WASHING

The eternal debate of whether to pre-wash will always have proponents on each side of the argument. Personally, we never pre-wash fabric. Fabric fresh off the bolt generally has a crisp feel and fewer wrinkles than something that has been washed and dried. Before cutting, we iron the fabric with a hot iron, steam and spray starch. This combination will generally reveal if any fabric is a candidate for excessive shrinking. Once a quilt is finished, dye catcher sheets such as the Shout Color Catcher can be thrown into the washing machine to catch any dye that isn't stable.

SEAM ALLOWANCE

Take time to make sure you are sewing with an accurate 1/4″ seam allowance. All the patterns in this book assume you are sewing with a 1/4″ seam allowance. One simple way to make sure you have an accurate seam allowance is to cut 3 strips 1 1/2″ x 9″. Sew them together. Measure the center strip. If it measures 1″ exactly, then your seam allowance is good to go! If not, try placing a piece of tape 1/4″ away from your needle in front

of your presser foot to use as a guide and try again. Continue experimenting with placement of the tape until that center strip is 1″ wide.

PRESSING

In general, press seams to the darker fabric. We like to press after each piecing step.

APPLIQUE

The templates provided in this book for appliquéd shapes show the finished edge of the piece as a solid line. Depending on your preferred method of appliqué, you can prepare templates and appliqué as desired. For this quilt, we used a very small machine buttonhole stitch to attach the appliqué shapes to the background. Refer to your local library or quilt shop for instruction books on any appliqué method.

TEMPLATES

To accurately piece some of the blocks, templates are required. To make them, trace the template onto freezer paper. Be sure to include the seam allowance if you are machine piecing. Press the freezer paper template to your fabric and cut out with scissors or a rotary cutter. Sew as usual.

3" x 89"

5⅞" x 9½"

3¼" x 9½"   3½" x 12½"

3" x 102½"   4" x 102½"

Note: These dimensions include seam allowance.

You will want to measure your quilt after piecing the columns to get the exact measurement to cut your sashing and border strips.

5⅞" x 9½"

CUTTING

When Aurelia drafted and pieced her blocks, she was not concerned with whether points matched or were chopped off. Because today's quilters have so many more options, accuracy has become more important. To make the blocks, not only fit but also to be accurate, some are written with the cutting measurements in 1/16″ increments rather than the more common 1/8″.

Traditional rulers show increments starting at 1/8″. The 1/16″ measurement falls halfway in between 1/8″ markings (see illustration). Prepare your fabric for cutting just as you normally do. The only difference is you will be counting out the 1/16″ lines on your ruler instead of the 1/8″ lines. Once cut, you will sew the same as usual, using your accurate 1/4″ seam allowance.

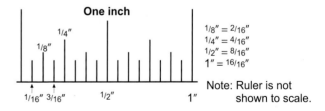

One inch

1/4″

1/8″

1/8″ = 2/16″
1/4″ = 4/16″
1/2″ = 8/16″
1″ = 16/16″

1/16″ 3/16″   1/2″   1″

Note: Ruler is not shown to scale.

A few rulers today are making an effort to include 1/16″ markings. A new entry on the market is Marsha McCloskey's Feathered Star Ruler. It has 1/16″ markings clearly marked, and we highly recommend it. You can find it on her website, **www.marshamccloskey.com**.

If you prefer, templates are also provided for each block in the back of the book.

CHAPTER 1

THE MISSOURI COMPROMISE OF 1820

In the early 1800s, Missouri existed as a large territory of the United States covering an area that would currently range from the Canadian border to Kansas and from Michigan to Idaho. Citizens in the area that roughly forms Missouri's current borders decided to petition Congress for Statehood in 1818. At that time, 22 states formed the Union, 11 of which were slave-holding states and 11 of which were anti-slavery. Then, as now, each state enjoyed two Senators so the division of power in the Senate was equal. However, in the House of Representatives, the population of a state determined the number of its representatives. Thus, the more heavily populated free North had an advantage over the less populated pro-slavery South.

When Missouri sought statehood, the perceived balance of power between the two sides was in jeopardy. A New York representative, James Tallmadge, proposed to allow Missouri into the Union only if slavery was banned in the state. At the time, residents of the territory held almost 2,000 slaves, a considerable number for the area. Tallmadge's proposal passed the House but could not move forward in the Senate so Missouri's bid for statehood stalled.

By 1820, a bill to admit Maine to the Union as a free state gained support in the House. This generated renewed interest in admitting Missouri to the Union as a slave state with the idea that admitting both territories would preserve the balance of an equal number of both free and slave-holding states in the overall Union. When the two proposals were merged in the Senate, Tallmadge's prohibition on slavery in Missouri was modified to prohibit slavery in the remainder of

> "A fire has been kindled which all the waters of the ocean cannot put out, and which only seas of blood can extinguish."
>
> — Comment by a Georgia representative as terms of the compromise were debated.

the Louisiana Purchase north of 36°30'N latitude, or roughly anything north of the southern boundary of Missouri.

Missouri's constitutional drafters then inserted language in their draft constitution prohibiting free blacks from moving into Missouri. This language angered Congressmen from the North who barred action on Missouri's status until Missouri legislators pledged not to include any language that would impair the rights of any citizen of the United States. The agreement barring slavery north of the 36°30'N latitude line remained intact for some 30 years. During that time, the Union would see a limitation on the growth of slave-holding states.

Missouri officially became the 24th state in the Union on August 10, 1821.

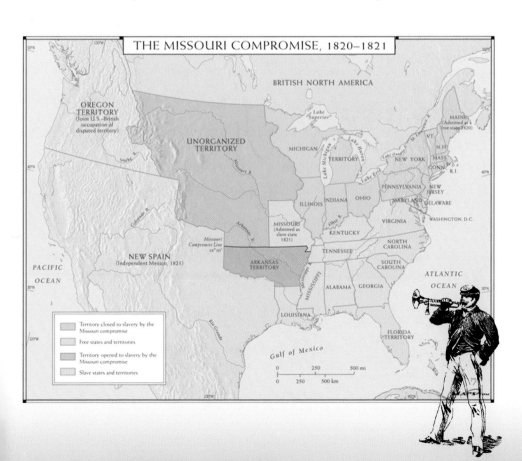

THE MISSOURI COMPROMISE, 1820–1821

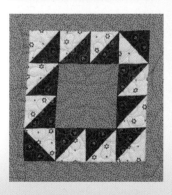

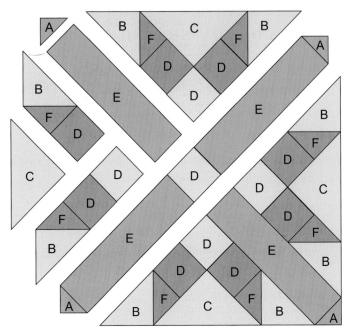

Block No. 1　　　　**FINISHED SIZE: 9″ SQUARE**

FABRICS REQUIRED: TWO BROWN PRINTS, LIGHT PRINT (BACKGROUND)
TEMPLATES ARE FOUND ON PAGE 72.

CUTTING

From brown print No. 1, cut:
   2 – 1 3/4″ squares. Cut each in
      half on the diagonal to yield
      4 A triangles.
   4 – 1 3/4″ x 5 9/16″ E rectangles.

From brown print No. 2, cut:
   8 – 1 3/4″ D squares.
   2 – 3″ squares. Cut on both
      diagonals to yield 8 F triangles.

From the background, cut:
   4 – 2 5/8″ squares. Cut each in half
      on the diagonal to yield
      8 B triangles.
   1 – 4 13/16″ square. Cut on both
      diagonals to yield 4 C triangles.
   5 – 1 3/4″ D squares.

PIECING

STAR POINT UNITS

Refer to the diagram for placement.

1. Sew 1 brown No. 2 F triangle to 1
   background B triangle. Make 4.
2. Sew 1 brown print No. 2 D square
   to the F triangle. Make 4
3. Sew 1 background D square to
   the brown print No. 2 D squares.
   Make 4.
4. Sew 1 brown No. 2 F triangle to 1
   background B triangle. This is the
   reverse image of Step 1. Make 4.
5. Sew 1 brown print No. 2 D square
   to the brown No. 2 F triangle.
6. Sew 1 background C triangle to the
   side of the short units. Make 4.

7. Sew these units to the side of the
   longer star point units made in
   Steps 1-3. Make 4.

RECTANGLE UNITS

8. Sew 1 brown No. 1 A triangle
   to one end of 4 brown No. 1 E
   rectangles.
9. Sew a rectangle unit in between
   two of the star point units. Make 2.

MIDDLE SECTION

10. Sew 2 rectangle units to 1 back
    ground D square.

BLOCK ASSEMBLY

11. Lay out 3 units and sew together as
    shown in the block diagram.

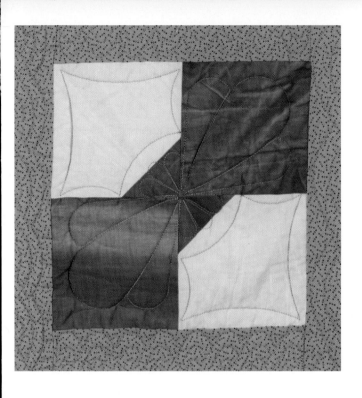

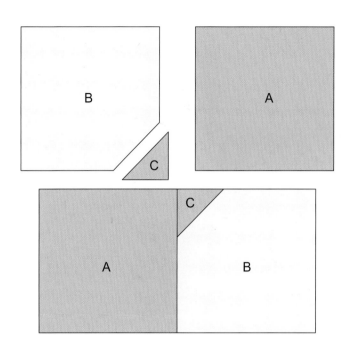

Block No. 2

FINISHED SIZE: 9″ SQUARE

FABRICS REQUIRED: BROWN SOLID, LIGHT PRINT (BACKGROUND)
TEMPLATES ARE FOUND ON PAGE 73-74.

CUTTING

From the brown solid, cut:
- 2 – 5″ A squares.
- 2 – 2 3/8″ C squares.

From the background, cut:
- 2 – 5″ B squares.

PIECING

Refer to the diagram for placement.

1. Press 1 C square in half on the diagonal. Open and place on the corner of 1 background B square.
2. Sew the small square to the large square using the pressed line as the guide. Trim excess off to 1/4″. Press small triangle to the outside to make 1 large square. Trim seam allowance. Make 2.

BLOCK ASSEMBLY

3. Lay out the 4 units and sew together as shown in the block diagram.

OHIO STAR

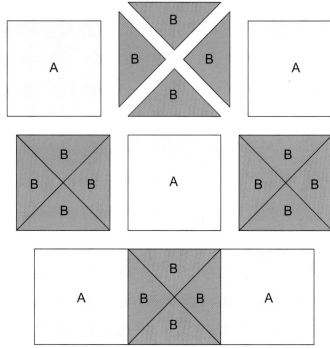

FINISHED SIZE: 9″ SQUARE

FABRICS REQUIRED: 2 DIFFERENT RED PRINTS, 2 DIFFERENT BROWN PRINTS, 2 DIFFERENT LIGHT PRINTS (BACKGROUNDS). THIS IS ENOUGH TO MAKE BLOCK NO. 3 AND BLOCK NO. 42. TEMPLATES ARE FOUND ON PAGE 74.

CUTTING

From each of the red prints, cut:
2 – 4 1/4″ squares. Cut on both diagonals to yield 8 B triangles.

From each of the brown prints, cut:
2 – 4 1/4″ squares. Cut on both diagonals to yield 8 B triangles.

From each of the backgrounds, cut:
5 – 3 1/2″ A squares.

PIECING

QUARTER-SQUARE TRIANGLE UNITS

Refer to the diagram for placement.

1. Sew the short sides of 1 red B triangle to 1 brown B triangle. Make 8. Be sure the red triangle is always on the same side of the brown triangle in all 8 units.

2. Sew two units together to form 1 quarter-square triangle unit. Make 4.

Rows

3. Sew 2 background A squares to either side of 1 quarter-square triangle unit. Make 2.

4. Sew 2 quarter square triangle units to either side of 1 background A square.

BLOCK ASSEMBLY

5. Sew the three rows together as shown in the block diagram. Repeat with the remaining fabrics to make block No. 42.

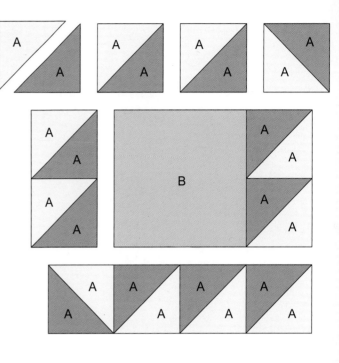

Block No. 4

FINISHED SIZE: 9″ SQUARE

FABRICS REQUIRED: RED PRINT, CHEDDAR PRINT, LIGHT PRINT (BACKGROUND)
TEMPLATES ARE FOUND ON PAGE 75.

CUTTING

From the red print, cut:
  6 – 3 1/8″ squares. Cut each on the
  diagonal to yield 12 A triangles.

From the cheddar print, cut:
  1 – 5″ B square.

From the background, cut:
  6 – 3 1/8″ squares. Cut each on the
  diagonal to yield 12 A triangles.

PIECING

HALF-SQUARE TRIANGLE UNITS

1. Sew 1 background A triangle to
   1 red A triangle to make 1 half-
   square triangle unit. Make 12.

ROWS

Refer to the diagram for placement.

2. Sew 4 half-square triangle units
   together in a row as shown in the
   diagram. Make 2.

3. Sew 2 half-square triangle units
   together. Make 2. Sew these units to
   either side of the cheddar B square.

BLOCK ASSEMBLY

4. Lay out the 3 rows and sew
   together as shown in the block
   diagram.

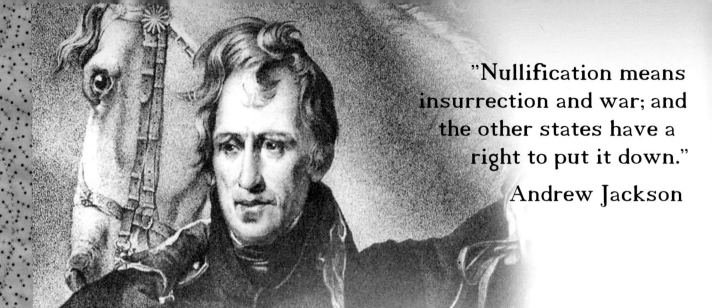

"Nullification means insurrection and war; and the other states have a right to put it down."

Andrew Jackson

CHAPTER 2

THE NULLIFICATION DOCTRINE, 1832

As the federal government took shape in the early 1800s, the issue of how much authority a central government could exercise over states developed. As states in the North developed more industry and moved away from an economy based in agriculture, the South began to feel that national policies favored the North. As a result, they argued that the federal government could only enact laws directly authorized by the United States Constitution. Southern states decided that any law that was beyond the scope of the Constitution could be declared void by the state.

The nullification crisis rose to a critical level when Congress enacted tariffs in 1828 and 1832 which the South felt favored northern manufacturing over southern agriculture. At the time, southern states sent a lot of their cotton overseas and in return purchased goods from European countries. Northern states wanted the South to purchase their goods instead, but they were not interested in exchanging those goods for the South's cotton. Congress responded by placing tariffs on the imported goods from Europe which they hoped would pressure the South to take goods from the North instead.

In response, South Carolina's state legislature declared that the tariffs were "unauthorized by the constitution of the United States, and violate the true meaning and intent thereof and are null, void, and no law, nor binding upon this State." President Andrew Jackson reacted quickly by issuing a proclamation that disputed a state's right to declare a federal law null.

would be poverty and utter desolation; her citizens, in despair, would emigrate to more fortunate regions, and the whole frame and constitution of her civil polity be impaired and deranged, if not dissolved entirely.

Deeply impressed with these considerations, the representatives of the good people of this commonwealth, anxiously desiring to live in peace with their fellow-citizens, and to do all that in them lies to preserve and perpetuate the union of the states, and liberties of which it is the surest pledge, but feeling it to be their bounden duty to expose and resist all encroachments upon the true spirit of the Constitution, lest an apparent acquiescence in the system of protecting duties should be drawn into precedent — do, in the name of the commonwealth of South Carolina, claim to enter upon the Journal of the Senate their *protest* against it as unconstitutional, oppressive, and unjust.

PRESIDENT JACKSON'S PROCLAMATION,

OF THE 10TH DECEMBER, 1833,

CONCERNING

THE ORDINANCE OF SOUTH CAROLINA. ON THE SUBJECT OF THE TARIFF,

ON THE 24TH NOVEMBER, 1832.

WHEREAS a convention assembled in the state of South Carolina have passed an ordinance, by which they declare "that the several acts, and parts of acts, of the Congress of the United States, purporting to be laws for the imposing duties and imposts on the importation of foreign commodities, and now having actual operation and effect within the United States," and more especially, two acts for the same purposes, passed on the 29th of May, 1828, and on the 14th of July, 1832, "are unauthorized by the Constitution of the United States, and violate the true meaning and intent thereof, and are null and void, and no law," not binding on the citizens of that state or its officers; and by the said ordinance it is further declared to be unlawful for any of the constituted authorities of the state, or of the United States, to enforce the payment of the duties imposed by the said acts within the same state, and that it is the duty of the legislature to pass such laws as may be necessary to give full effect to the said ordinance:

And whereas, by the said ordinance, it is further ordained, that, in any case of law or equity decided in the courts of said state, wherein shall be drawn in question the validity of the said ordinance, or of the acts of the legislature that may be passed to give it effect, or of the said laws of the United States, no appeal shall be allowed to the Supreme Court of the United States, nor shall any copy of the record be permitted or allowed for that purpose, and that any person attempting to take such appeal shall be punished as for a contempt of court:

And, finally, the said ordinance declares that the people of South Carolina will maintain the said ordinance at every hazard; and that they will consider the passage of any act, by abolishing or closing the ports of the

Congress also responded by passing the Force Act which authorized military troops to enforce revenue laws. Hoping to avoid a crisis, Congress then negotiated a change in the tariffs which would slowly lower the tariffs over a 10-year period. South Carolina agreed to this compromise and further dispute about whether a state could object to a federal law was avoided.

The issue would return in the 1860s when states began contemplating secession from the Union in response to anti-slavery laws.

DEVIL'S CLAW

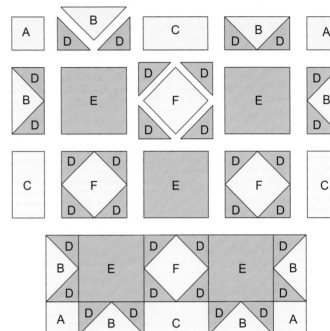

Block No. 5

FINISHED SIZE: 9″ SQUARE

FABRICS REQUIRED: BLUE PRINT, LIGHT PRINT (BACKGROUND)
TEMPLATES ARE FOUND ON PAGE 75.

CUTTING

From the blue print, cut:
- 16 – 2″ squares. Cut each in half on the diagonal to make 32 D triangles.
- 5 – 2 3/4″ E squares.

From the background, cut:
- 4 – 1 5/8″ A squares.
- 2 – 3 1/2″ squares. Cut on both diagonals to yield 8 B triangles.
- 4 - 1 5/8″ x 2 3/4″ C rectangles.
- 4 – 2 1/16″ F squares.

PIECING

FLYING GEESE UNITS

Refer to the diagram for placement.

1. Sew 2 blue D triangles to either side of 1 background B triangle to make a flying geese unit. Make 8.

SQUARE-IN-A-SQUARE UNITS

2. Sew 2 blue D triangles to opposite sides of 1 background F square. Sew 2 more blue D triangles to the remaining 2 sides of the square. Make 4.

Rows

3. Lay out 2 background A squares, 2 flying geese units and 1 background C rectangle. Sew together in a row. Make 2.

4. Lay out 2 flying geese units, two blue E squares and 1 square-in-a-square unit. Sew together in a row. Make 2.

5. Lay out remaining 2 background C rectangles, 2 square-in-a-square units and 1 blue E square. Make 1.

BLOCK ASSEMBLY

6. Lay out the 5 rows and sew together as shown in the block diagram.

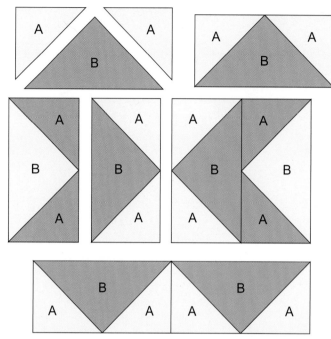

Block No. 6 and 38

FINISHED SIZE: 9″ SQUARE

FABRICS REQUIRED: 2 DIFFERENT BROWN PRINTS, 2 DIFFERENT LIGHT PRINTS (BACKGROUNDS). THIS IS ENOUGH TO MAKE BLOCK NO. 6 AND BLOCK NO. 38. TEMPLATES ARE FOUND ON PAGE 76.

CUTTING

From each of the brown print, cut:
- 2 – 3 1/8″ squares. Cut each in half on the diagonal to yield 4 A triangles
- 2 – 5 3/4″ square. Cut in half on the diagonal twice to yield 8 B triangles. You will use only 6 brown B triangles per block.

From each of the background, cut:
- 6 – 3 1/8″ squares. Cut each in half on the diagonal to yield 12 A triangles
- 1 – 5 3/4″ squares. Cut in half on both diagonals to yield 4 B triangles. You will use only 2 background B triangles per block.

PIECING

FLYING GEESE UNITS

Refer to the diagram for placement.

1. Sew 2 brown A triangles to either side of 1 background B triangle to make a flying geese unit. Make 2.

2. Sew 2 background A triangles to either side of 1 brown B triangle to make a flying geese unit. Make 6.

BLOCK ASSEMBLY

3. Lay out flying geese and sew together shown in the block diagram. Repeat with the remaining fabrics to make block No. 38.

WANDERING LOVER

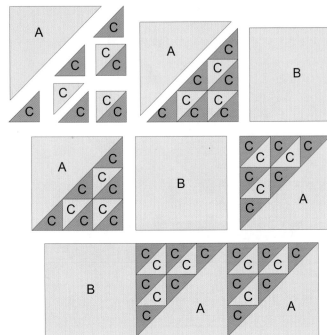

FINISHED SIZE: 9″ SQUARE

FABRICS REQUIRED: PINK PRINT, LIGHT PRINT (BACKGROUND)
TEMPLATES ARE FOUND ON PAGE 76.

CUTTING

From the pink print, cut:

- 18 – 1 7/8″ squares. Cut each in half on the diagonal to yield 36 C triangles.

From the background, cut:

- 3 – 3 7/8″ squares. Cut each in half on the diagonal to yield 6 A triangles.
- 3 – 3 1/2″ B squares.
- 9 – 1 7/8″ squares. Cut each in half on the diagonal to yield 18 C triangles.

PIECING

HALF-SQUARE TRIANGLE UNITS

Refer to the diagram for placement.

1. Sew 1 pink C triangle to 1 background C triangle to make a half-square triangle unit. Make 18.

PIECED TRIANGLE UNITS

2. Lay out three half square triangles and three pink C triangles. Sew together to form a pieced triangle unit. Make 6.

LARGE HALF-SQUARE TRIANGLE UNITS

3. Lay out 1 pieced triangle unit and 1 background A triangle unit. Sew together. Make 6.

BLOCK ASSEMBLY

4. Lay out the pieced units and 3 background B squares and sew together as shown in the block diagram.

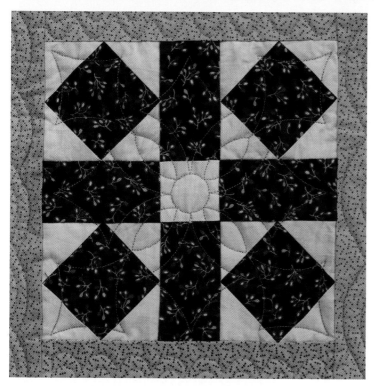

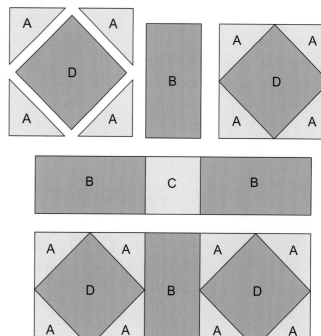

Block No. 8

FINISHED SIZE: 9″ SQUARE

FABRICS REQUIRED: BROWN PRINT, LIGHT PRINT (BACKGROUND)
TEMPLATES ARE FOUND ON PAGE 77.

CUTTING

From the brown print, cut:
  4 – 2 5/16″ x 4 1/8″ B rectangles.
  4 – 3 1/16″ D squares.

From the background, cut:
  8 – 2 5/8″ squares. Cut each in half
    on the diagonal to yield 16 A
    triangles.
  1 – 2 5/16″ C square.

PIECING

SQUARE-IN-A-SQUARE UNITS

Refer to the diagram for placement.

1. Sew 2 background A triangles to
   opposite sides of 1 brown print D
   square. Sew 2 more background A
   triangles to remaining sides of the
   brown print D square. Make 4.

ROWS

2. Lay out 1 brown print B rectangle
   and 2 square-in-a-square units as
   shown in the diagram. Sew together
   in a row. Make 2.

3. Lay out 2 brown print B rectangles
   and 1 background C square as
   shown in the diagram. Sew together
   in a row. Make 1.

BLOCK ASSEMBLY

4. Lay out the three rows and sew
   together as shown in the block
   diagram.

CHAPTER 3

THE COMPROMISE OF 1850 AND THE FUGITIVE SLAVE ACT

As the United States continued to expand westward, the issue of whether certain areas would be designated free states or slave-holding states remained controversial. The nullification controversy surrounding the tariffs of 1828 and 1832 underscored for those in the South that they had to retain their balance of power in the United States Senate to preserve their rights. Therefore, any effort to add territories as states was met with much suspicion and hostility from the South.

In 1850, California was ready to join the Union and prevailing sentiment clearly dictated it would be a free state. Abolitionists in the North also wanted an end to the slave market that existed in Washington, D.C. In addition, Texas and lands to its west sought recognition as official territories of the United States. Congress sought to deal with all of these issues by adopting a group of five bills known as the Compromise of 1850, engineered by Senator Henry Clay of Kentucky. To secure support from the South, one of these bills was the Fugitive Slave Act, designed to strengthen slave-owners' rights with regard to their slaves. The law specifically empowered a group of federal commissioners to pursue slaves across any state boundary, without any statute of limitation. In effect, a slave could escape, establish a life in a free state and live for many years, then be captured by a federal commissioner and returned to slavery without any hearing or due process. Other components of the Compromise provided that California would be designated a free state while the newly recognized territories of New Mexico and Utah would use the popular sovereignty concept to determine their own fate. Texas, which had earlier sought to include New Mexico within its boundaries, was given $10 million by the federal government to pay off its debt to the country of Mexico. Finally, the slave market in the District of Columbia was abolished, however, individuals in that area could still own slaves.

The compromise was designed to soothe tensions between the North and South and avoid splitting the Union. The effect was exactly the opposite. Abolitionists were appalled that free men could be rounded up and returned to a life of captivity without any chance to defend themselves. Southerners were unhappy that additional areas had joined the Union as free or undecided areas. Ultimately, the Compromise of 1850 merely added to the simmering tensions among the states.

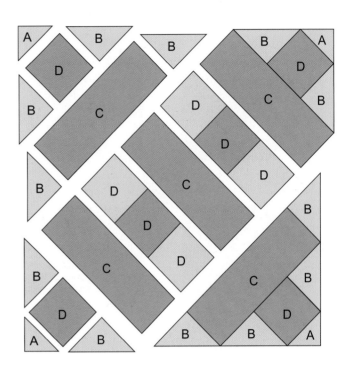

Block No. 9

FINISHED SIZE: 12″ SQUARE

FABRICS REQUIRED: CHEDDAR PRINT, RED PRINT
TEMPLATES ARE FOUND ON PAGE 78.

CUTTING

From the cheddar print, cut:

- 2 – 2 3/8″ squares. Cut each in half on the diagonal to yield 4 A triangles.
- 3 – 4 1/4″ squares. Cut on both diagonals to yield 12 B triangles.
- 4 – 2 5/8″ D squares.

From the red print, cut:

- 6 – 2 5/8″ D squares.
- 5 – 2 5/8″ x 6 7/8″ C rectangles.

PIECING

CORNER TRIANGLE UNITS

Refer to the diagram for placement.

1. Lay out 1 red D square, 1 red C rectangle, 4 cheddar B triangles and 1 cheddar A triangle. Sew 2 cheddar B triangles to either side of 1 red D square. Sew 1 cheddar A triangle to the top. Sew 1 red C rectangle to the bottom. Sew the remaining cheddar B triangles to either side of the red C rectangle. Make 2.

MIDDLE SECTION

2. Lay out 1 red D square, 2 cheddar B triangles, 1 cheddar A triangle and 1 red C rectangle. Sew 2 cheddar B triangles to either side of 1 red D square. Add 1 cheddar A triangle to the top and the red C rectangle to the bottom. Make 2.

3. Sew 2 cheddar D squares to either side of 1 red D square. Make 2.

4. Lay out the remaining red C rectangle and the 2 units from Step 3. Sew together.

BLOCK ASSEMBLY

3. Lay out the 3 sections and sew together as shown in the block diagram.

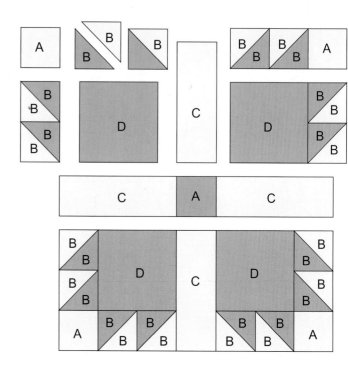

Block No. 10

FINISHED SIZE: 12″ SQUARE

FABRICS REQUIRED: BLACK PRINT, LIGHT PRINT (BACKGROUND)
TEMPLATES ARE FOUND ON PAGE 79.

CUTTING

From the black print, cut:
- 1 – 2 1/4″ A square.
- 8 – 2 9/16″ squares. Cut each in half on the diagonal to yield 16 B triangles.
- 4 – 3 15/16″ D squares.

From the background, cut:
- 4 – 2 1/4″ A squares.
- 8 – 2 9/16″ squares. Cut each in half on the diagonal to yield 16 B triangles
- 4 – 2 1/4″ x 5 5/8″ C rectangles.

PIECING

HALF-SQUARE TRIANGLE UNITS

Refer to the diagram for placement.

1. Sew 1 B background triangle to 1 B black triangle to form 1 half-square triangle unit. Make 16.

BEAR PAW UNITS

2. Sew 2 half-square triangle units together. Make 4.

3. Sew 2 half-square triangle units together going in the opposite direction. Make 4. Make sure this section group of 4 is the mirror image of the first group of 4. To this second group, sew 1 background A square to the end.

4. Sew the first group of half-square triangles to the side of 1 black D square. Sew the second group to the top. Pay attention to placement to make sure the half-square triangle units are facing the correct direction. Make 4.

ROWS

5. Lay out 2 Bear paw units and 1 background C rectangle. Sew together in a row. Make 2.

6. Lay out 2 background C rectangles and 1 black A square. Sew together in a row. Make 1.

BLOCK ASSEMBLY

7. Lay out the 3 rows and sew together as shown in the block diagram.

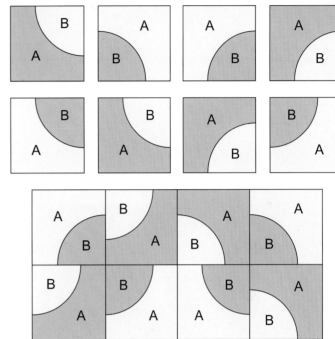

Block No. 11

FINISHED SIZE: 12″ SQUARE

FABRICS REQUIRED: BROWN PRINT, AGED MUSLIN (BACKGROUND)
TEMPLATES ARE FOUND ON PAGE 79.

CUTTING

From the brown print, cut:
   8 – pieces from Template A.
   8 – pieces from Template B.

From the muslin, cut:
   8 – pieces from Template A.
   8 – pieces from Template B.

PIECING

Refer to the diagram for placement.

1. Sew 1 brown print Template A to 1 muslin Template B as shown in the diagram. Make 8.

2. Sew 1 brown print Template B to 1 muslin Template A as shown in the diagram. Make 8.

Piecing tip: To make the square, pinning is very important. Start by pinning a Template B to a Template A starting at the left hand corner and pinning around the curve to the right hand side.

BLOCK ASSEMBLY

1. Lay out all 16 squares and sew together as shown in the block diagram.

HOUSE

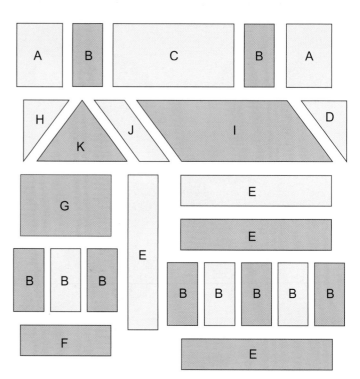

FINISHED SIZE: 12″ SQUARE

FABRICS REQUIRED: BLUE PRINT, LIGHT TAN (BACKGROUND)
TEMPLATES ARE FOUND ON PAGE 80-81.

CUTTING

From the blue print, cut:
  7 – 1 13/16″ x 3 3/16″ B rectangles.
  2 – 1 13/16″ x 7 3/16″ E rectangles.
  1 – 1 13/16″ x 4 1/2″ F rectangle.
  1 – 3 3/16″ x 4 1/2″ G rectangle.
  1 – I template.
  1 – K template.

From the background, cut:
  2 – 2 1/2″ x 3 3/16″ A rectangles.
  3 – 1 13/16″ x 3 3/16″ B rectangles.
  1 – 3 3/16″ x 5 13/16″ C rectangle.
  1 – D template.
  2 – 1 13/16″ x 7 3/16″ E rectangles.
  1 – H template.
  1 – J template.

PIECING

Refer to the diagram for placement.
To make the House block you will
make four sections.

1. Lay out 2 background A rectangles,
   2 blue print B rectangles and 1
   background C rectangle and sew
   together.

2. Lay out the H, K, J, I and D
   templates and sew together.

3. Sew 2 blue B rectangles to either
   side of 1 background B rectangle.
   Sew the blue print G rectangle to
   the top of this unit. Sew the blue
   print F rectangle to the bottom
   of this unit and 1 background E
   rectangle to the right.

4. Starting with the blue, sew 3 blue
   B rectangles alternating with 2
   background B rectangles in a row.
   Sew 2 blue E rectangles to the top
   and bottom of this unit. Sew the
   background E rectangle to the top
   of this unit.

BLOCK ASSEMBLY

5. Lay out the 4 sections and sew
   together as shown in the block
   diagram.

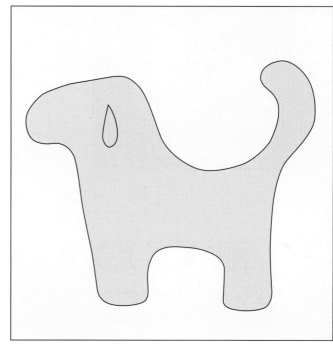

Block No. 13

FINISHED SIZE: 12″ SQUARE

FABRICS REQUIRED: TAN PRINT, AGED MUSLIN (BACKGROUND)
TEMPLATE IS ON PAGE 82.

CUTTING

From the tan print, cut:
  1 – dog shape from template.
  1 - ear shape

From the muslin, cut:
  1 – 13 1/2″ square.

APPLIQUE

Referring to the photo for placement, appliqué the dog shape to the center of the background square. Use the method of your choice. Trim block to 12 1/2″ after sewing.

While political and military events were moving the country toward war, the publication of a book also had a strong impact on the country's sentiment. Harriet Beecher Stowe published Uncle Tom's Cabin in 1852. Stowe was born in Connecticut in 1811 to a prominent preacher. The Beecher family moved to Ohio in 1832 and lived near the Kentucky border. Harriet soon began teaching at a school for former slave children and frequently witnessed runaway slaves being pursued by bounty hunters. Then, in 1849, her sixth child, Samuel fell victim to a cholera epidemic. Medicine at the time did not even understand what cholera was so Harriet was forced to stand by and watch her child slowly die. The experience profoundly changed her. Suddenly, Harriet felt like she could understand how horrible it was for a slave woman to have her child taken from her.

CHAPTER 4

PUBLICATION OF UNCLE TOM'S CABIN, 1852

Soon after Samuel's death, Congress passed the Fugitive Slave Act. Northerners who had previously avoided taking a position on slavery had to decide what they would do if they saw a fugitive slave. So, when Harriet returned to New England in 1850, she resolved to write something that would show the suffering of the slaves and perhaps incite others to take action on their behalf. Harriet commented: "Up to this year I have always felt that I had no particular call to meddle with this subject, and I dreaded to expose even my own mind to the full force of its exciting power. But I feel now that the time is come when even a woman or a child who can speak a word for freedom and humanity is bound to speak. The Carthagenian women in the last peril of their state cut off their hair for bow strings to give to the defenders of their country, and such peril and shame as now hangs over this country is worse than Roman slavery, and I hope every woman who can write will not be silent."

Originally Harriet's story began as a serialized feature in the "National Era," a newspaper in Washington, D.C., running from June 5, 1851 to August 1, 1852. The series grew in popularity over this time period so when the stories were collected into a two-volume book published on March 20, 1852, more than 10,000 copies sold in just two weeks.

Written from the perspective of Uncle Tom, a devout slave who was owned by many masters, the story depicts the suffering and abuse of slaves culminating with Tom being beaten to death by his last owner. Through it all, Tom remains faithful and even prays that his master will repent and be saved as he is dying.

By 1856, more than 2 million copies of the book had been sold and Harriet's desired firestorm was underway. Southerners reacted with outrage proclaiming that the book exaggerated the plight of the slaves. Harriet responded by printing a collection of narratives and newspaper clippings that documented some of the abuses occurring in the South.

Today, critics fault Uncle Tom's Cabin for perpetuating many negative stereotypes about blacks. The narrative contains descriptions of a lazy "happy darky" and affectionate "mammies." However, the impact of the book at the time of its publication can not be underestimated. The book became an international bestseller. So many readers in England were impacted by the stories of abuse that Britain ultimately declined to aid the South when the war started. President Abraham Lincoln even acknowledged the book's impact when he met Harriet by commenting that Stowe was "the little woman that wrote the book that started this great war."

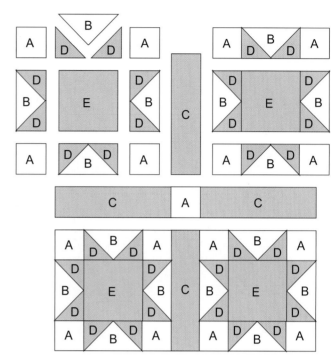

Block No. 14

FINISHED SIZE: 12″ SQUARE

FABRICS REQUIRED: BROWN PRINT, LIGHT PRINT (BACKGROUND)
TEMPLATES ARE FOUND ON PAGE 84.

CUTTING

From the brown print, cut:
- 4 – 1 13/16″ x 5 13/16″ C rectangles.
- 16 – 2 3/16″ squares. Cut each one on the diagonal to yield 32 D triangles.
- 4 – 3 3/16″ E squares.

From the background, cut:
- 17 – 1 13/16″ A squares.
- 4 – 3 7/8″ squares. Cut on both diagonals to yield 16 B triangles.

PIECING

FLYING GEESE UNITS

Refer to the diagram for placement.
To make each star unit start by making your flying geese.
1. Sew 2 brown D triangles to either side of 1 background B triangle. Make 16.

STAR UNITS

2. Sew 2 background A squares to either side of 1 flying geese unit. Make 8.
3. Sew 2 flying geese units to either side of 1 brown E square. Make 4.
4. Sew these units together in rows. Make 4.

ROWS

5. Sew 2 star units to either side of 1 brown C rectangle. Make 2.
6. Sew 2 brown C rectangles to either side of 1 background A square. Make 1.

BLOCK ASSEMBLY

7. Lay out the rows and sew together as shown in the block diagram

DEVIL'S FOOTPRINT

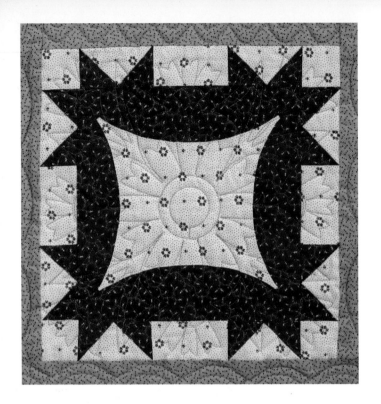

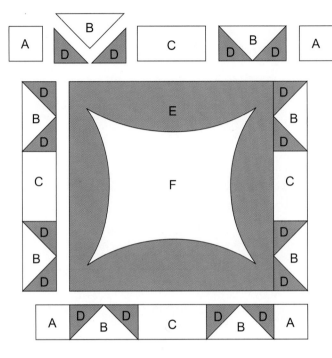

Block No. 15

FINISHED SIZE: 12″ SQUARE

FABRICS REQUIRED: RED PRINT, LIGHT PRINT (BACKGROUND)
TEMPLATES ARE FOUND ON PAGE 85-86.

CUTTING

From the red print, cut:
- 8 – 2 3/8″ squares. Cut each in half on the diagonal to yield 16 D triangles.
- 1 – 9 1/2″ E square.

From the background, cut:
- 4 – 2″ A squares.
- 2 – 4 1/4″ squares. Cut on both diagonals to yield 8 B triangles.
- 4 – 2″ x 3 1/2″ C rectangles.
- 1 – F template.

PIECING

FLYING GEESE UNITS

Refer to the diagram for placement.

1. Sew 2 red D triangles to either side of 1 background B triangle as shown in the diagram. Make 8.

APPLIQUÉ

2. Referring to the diagram for placement, appliqué the background F template to the red E square. Use the appliqué method of your choice.

Rows

3. Lay out 2 background A squares, 2 flying geese units and 1 background C rectangle and sew together. Make 2.

4. Lay out 2 flying geese units and 1 background C rectangle and sew together. Make 2. Sew these to either side of the appliqué unit. Be sure they are placed properly.

BLOCK ASSEMBLY

5. Lay out the rows and sew together as shown in the block diagram

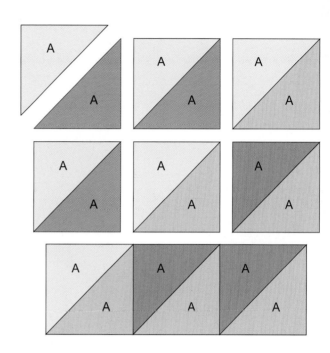

Block No. 16

FINISHED SIZE: 12″ SQUARE

FABRICS REQUIRED: PINK PRINT, BROWN PRINT, RED PRINT, BLACK PRINT
TEMPLATES IS FOUND ON PAGE 89.

CUTTING

From the pink print, cut:
- 3 – 4 7/8″ squares. Cut each in half on the diagonal to yield 6 Piece A triangles.

From the brown print, cut:
- 3 – 4 7/8″ squares. Cut each in half on the diagonal to yield 6 Piece A triangles.

From the red print, cut:
- 2 – 4 7/8″ squares. Cut each in half on the diagonal to yield 3 Piece A triangles (discard one triangle).

From the black print, cut:
- 2 – 4 7/8″ squares. Cut each in half on the diagonal to yield 3 Piece A triangles (discard one triangle).

PIECING

HALF-SQUARE TRIANGLE UNITS

Refer to the diagram for placement.
1. Sew 1 pink A triangle to 1 red A triangle. Make 3.
2. Sew 1 pink A triangle to 1 brown A triangle. Make 3.
3. Sew 1 brown A triangle to 1 black A triangle. Make 3.

Rows

4. Lay out 2 Step 1 units and 1 Step 2 unit and sew together.
5. Lay out 1 Step 1 unit and 1 Step 2 unit and 1 Step 3 unit and sew together.
6. Lay out 1 Step 2 unit and 2 Step 3 units and sew together.

BLOCK ASSEMBLY

7. Lay out the rows and sew together as shown in the block diagram.

MINI BOWS

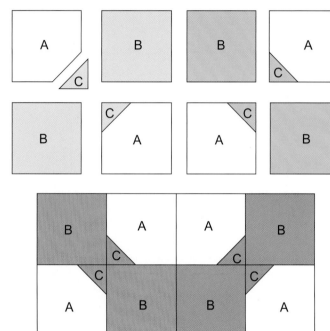

FINISHED SIZE: 12″ SQUARE

FABRICS REQUIRED: PINK PRINT, BLUE PRINT, BLACK PRINT, RED PRINT, LIGHT PRINT (BACKGROUND) TEMPLATES ARE FOUND ON PAGE 86.

CUTTING

From the pink print, cut:
  2 – 3 1/2″ B squares.
  2 – 2 1/8″ C squares.

From the blue print, cut:
  2 – 3 1/2″ B squares.
  2 – 2 1/8″ C squares.

From the black print, cut:
  2 – 3 1/2″ B squares.
  2 – 2 1/8″ C squares.

From the red print, cut:
  2 – 3 1/2″ B squares.
  2 – 2 1/8″ C squares.

From the background, cut:
  8 – 3 1/2″ A squares.

PIECING

Refer to the diagram for placement.

1. Press 1 C square in half on the diagonal. Open and place on the corner of 1 background square.

2. Sew the small square to the large square using the pressed line as the guide. Trim excess off to 1/4″. Press small triangle open to make 1 large square. Make 8, 2 of each color.

BOW TIE UNITS

3. Lay out 2 pink B squares and 2 pink background squares. Sew together as a four-patch block. Repeat with the remaining 3 colors.

BLOCK ASSEMBLY

3. Lay out the 4 units and sew together as shown in the block diagram.

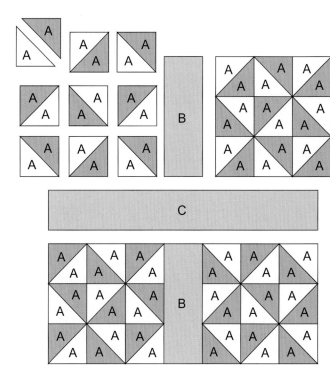

Block No. 18

FINISHED SIZE: 12″ SQUARE

FABRICS REQUIRED: 4 BROWN PRINTS, LIGHT PRINT (BACKGROUND)
TEMPLATES ARE FOUND ON PAGE 87.

CUTTING

From brown print No. 1, cut:
   9 – 2 9/16″ squares. Cut each in half on the diagonal to yield 18 A triangles.

From brown print No. 2, cut:
   9 – 2 9/16″ squares. Cut each in half on the diagonal to yield 18 A triangles.

From brown print No. 3, cut:
   2 – 2 3/8″ x 5 9/16″ B rectangles.

From brown print No. 4, cut:
   1 – 2 3/8″ x 12 1/2″ C rectangle.

From the background, cut:
   18 – 2 9/16″ squares. Cut each in half on the diagonal to yield 36 A triangles.

PIECING

HALF-SQUARE TRIANGLE UNITS

Refer to the diagram for placement.

1. Sew 1 brown print No. 1 A triangle to 1 background A triangle to make 1 half-square triangle unit. Make 18.

2. Sew 1 brown print No. 2 A triangle to 1 background A triangle to make 1 half-square triangle unit. Make 18.

3. Referring to the diagram, lay out the half-square triangle units and sew into 4 pieced units. Make sure all the half-square triangle units are placed correctly.

Rows

4. Sew 2 pieced units to either side of 1 Brown No. 3 B rectangle. Make 2.

BLOCK ASSEMBLY

5. Lay out the 3 rows and sew together as shown in the block diagram.

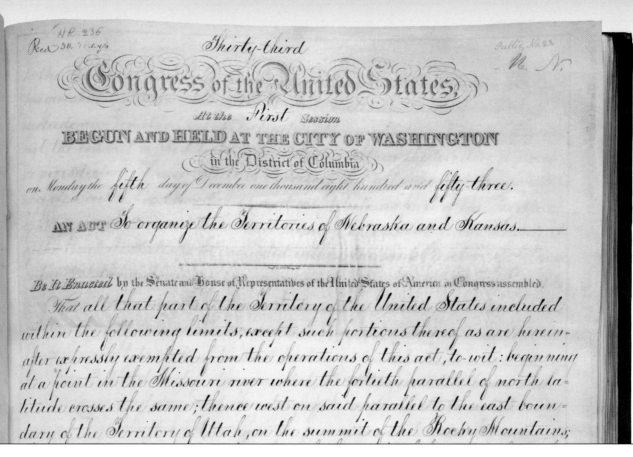

CHAPTER 5

THE KANSAS-NEBRASKA ACT OF 1854 'POPULAR SOVEREIGNTY'

By the 1850s pressure to allow slavery north of the 36°30'N line and in new territories like Texas and California was growing. Illinois Congressman Stephen Douglas wanted railroad lines to run from Chicago in his home state all the way to California, but before that could happen, the territories had to be organized and brought into the Union. So, Douglas crafted the Kansas-Nebraska Act, enacted on May 30, 1854, which allowed people in the territories of Kansas and Nebraska to decide whether to allow slavery within their borders. This concept was known as "popular sovereignty" since it would allow the residents of the area to decide whether to allow slavery.

The Act effectively repealed the Missouri Compromise of 1820 which had prohibited slavery north of latitude 36°30'N.

The Kansas-Nebraska Act proved especially divisive. Those in the North viewed the Missouri Compromise as a long-standing, binding agreement. Those in the pro-slavery South welcomed the chance to expand the count of slave-holding states.

Settlers on both sides of the issue rushed to claim land in Kansas prior to the first election on the slavery question. Voters opted to allow slavery in Kansas, but the anti-slavery faction claimed voting fraud.

We are not one people. We are two peoples. We are a people for Freedom and a people for Slavery. Between the two, conflict is inevitable.

— New York Tribune publisher Horace Greeley
on the Kansas Nebraska Act, 1854

Those opposed to slavery chose to have another election but the pro-slavery settlers refused to participate which resulted in Kansas having two separate, competing legislatures for a period of time. The two sides became violent and both suffered casualties. Fighting grew so intense that New York Times editor Horace Greeley christened the area "Bleeding Kansas."

President Franklin Pierce then sent Federal troops to Kansas in an effort to eliminate the anti-slavery legislature. A third election was held with the pro-slavery side prevailing amid renewed allegations of election fraud. Congress then chose not to recognize the resulting constitution meaning Kansas remained a territory.

By 1860, additional settlers had arrived in Kansas who tilted the sentiment in the state towards anti-slavery. Legislators drafted a new constitution which Congress recognized. Kansas was finally granted statehood on January 29, 1861, as a free state.

Opponents of the Kansas-Nebraska Act soon organized officially into the Republican Party. Even more importantly, a former politician was drawn back into public life as a result of the Act. Abraham Lincoln served one term in Congress in the 1840s before returning to Illinois. He had a long history with Stephen Douglas, beginning in the 1830s when both served in the state legislature. Lincoln was so upset by Douglas' legislative actions that he began speaking out against Douglas at public meetings. The two continued sparring publicly for many years as the country continued down the path that would lead to a war between the states.

"I deny the right of Congress to force a slaveholding State upon an unwilling people. I deny their right to force a free State upon an unwilling people. I deny their right to force a good thing upon a people who are unwilling to receive it. The great principle is the right of every community to judge and decide for itself, whether a thing if right or wrong, whether it would be good or evil for them to adopt it; and the right of free action, the right of free thought, the right of free judgment upon the question if dearer to every true American than any other under a free government."

— Democratic Senator Stephen A. Douglas, in a
speech delivered in Chicago, Illinois, July 1858

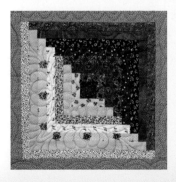

FOUR SQUARE

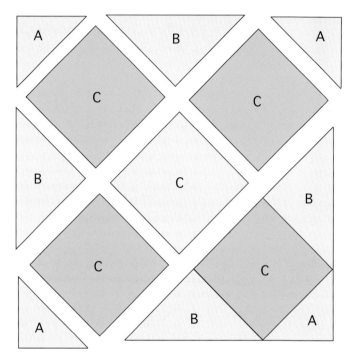

Block No. 19

FINISHED SIZE: 12″ SQUARE

FABRICS REQUIRED: RED PRINT, LIGHT PRINT (BACKGROUND)
TEMPLATES ARE FOUND ON PAGE 88.

CUTTING

From the red, cut:
  4 – 4 3/4″ C squares.

From the background, cut:
  2 – 3 7/8″ squares. Cut each on the
    diagonal to yield 4 A triangles.
  1 – 7 1/4″ square. Cut on both
    diagonals to yield 4 B triangles.
  1 – 4 3/4″ C square.

PIECING

Rows

1. Sew 2 background B triangles to
   either side of 1 red C square. Sew 1
   background A triangle to the top of
   this unit. Make 2.

2. Sew 2 red C squares to either side
   of 1 background C square. Sew 2 A
   triangles to either side of this unit.

BLOCK ASSEMBLY

3. Lay out the 3 rows and sew together as shown in the block diagram.

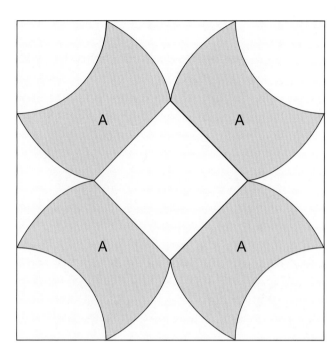

Block No. 20

FINISHED SIZE: 12″ SQUARE

FABRICS REQUIRED: BROWN PRINT, LIGHT PRINT (BACKGROUND)
TEMPLATE IS FOUND ON PAGE 89.

CUTTING

From the brown print, cut:
   4 – from A templates.

From the background, cut:
   1 – 13 1/2″ square.

APPLIQUE

Referring to the photo for placement, appliqué the 4 shapes to the background square. Use the appliqué method of your choice. Trim block to 12 1/2″ after sewing.

Note: Fold the background fabric in half and half again and lightly finger press to form registration marks to aid placement. When placing the applique shapes on the background, be careful not to place them in the seam allowance.

CARTWHEEL

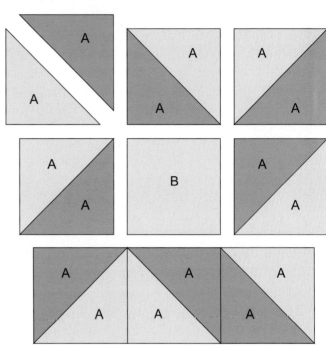

FINISHED SIZE: 12″ SQUARE

FABRICS REQUIRED: RED PRINT, CHEDDAR PRINT
TEMPLATES ARE FOUND ON PAGE 90.

CUTTING

From the red, cut:
- 4 – 4 7/8″ squares. Cut each in half on the diagonal to yield 8 A triangles.

From the cheddar, cut:
- 4 – 4 7/8″ squares. Cut each in half on the diagonal to yield 8 A triangles.
- 1 – 4 1/2″ B square.

PIECING

HALF-SQUARE TRIANGLE UNITS

1. Sew 1 red A triangle to 1 cheddar A triangle to make 1 half-square triangle unit. Make 8.

ROWS

Refer to diagram for placement.

2. Sew 3 half-square triangle units together. Make 2

3. Sew 2 half-square triangle units to either side of 1 B square.

BLOCK ASSEMBLY

4. Lay out the 3 rows and sew together as shown in the block diagram.

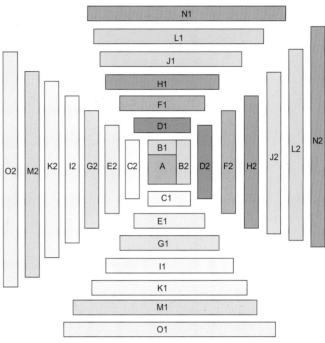

Block No. 22

FINISHED SIZE: 12″ SQUARE

FABRICS REQUIRED: 7 LIGHT PRINTS, 7 DARK PRINTS, RED PRINT
TEMPLATES ARE NOT GIVEN FOR THIS BLOCK. USE THE ROTARY CUTTING INSTRUCTIONS BELOW.

CUTTING

All strips are cut 1 1/4″ wide.

From the red print, cut:
1 – 2″ A square.

From a dark print, cut:
1 – 2″ B1 strip.
1 – 2 3/4″ B2 strip.

From a light print, cut:
1 – 2 3/4″ C1 strip.
1 – 3 1/2″ C2 strip.

From a dark print, cut:
1 – 3 1/2″ D1 strip.
1 – 4 1/4″ D2 strip.

From a light print, cut:
1 – 4 1/4″ E1 strip.
1 – 5″ E2 strip.

From a dark print, cut:
1 – 5″ F1 strip.
1 – 5 3/4″ F2 strip.

From a light print, cut:
1 – 5 3/4″ G1 strip.
1 – 6 1/2″ G2 strip.

From a dark print, cut:
1 – 6 1/2″ H1 strip.
1 – 7 1/4″ H2 strip.

From a light print, cut:
1 – 7 1/4″ I1 strip.
1 – 8″ I2 strip.

From a dark print, cut:
1 – 8″ J1 strip.
1 – 8 3/4″ J2 strip.

From a light print, cut:
1 – 8 3/4″ K1 strip.
1 – 9 1/2″ K2 strip.

From a dark print, cut:
1 – 9 1/2″ L1 strip.
1 – 10 1/4″ L2 strip.

From a light print, cut:
1 – 10 1/4″ M1 strip.
1 – 11″ M2 strip.

From a dark print, cut:
1 – 11″ N1 strip.
1 – 11 3/4″ N2 strip.

From a light print, cut:
1 – 11 3/4″ O1 strip.
1 – 12 1/2″ O2 strip.

PIECING

Refer to the diagram for placement. Sew the dark B1 strip to the top of the red A square. Next, sew the B2 strip to the right side of this unit. Continue working around the square with the next light C strip, and so forth, in alphabetical order, until the block is complete and matches the diagram.

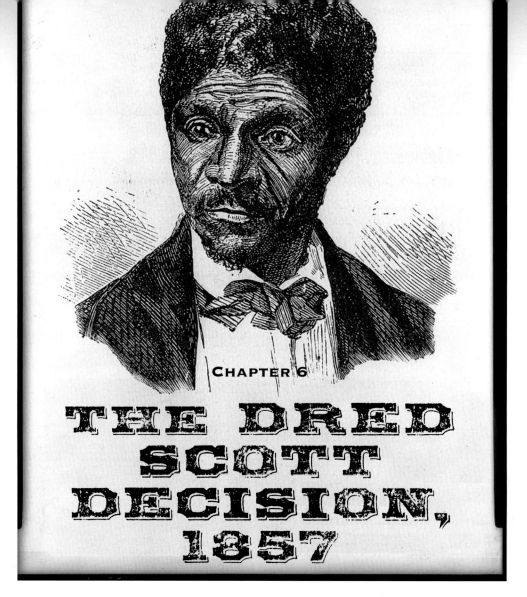

CHAPTER 6

THE DRED SCOTT DECISION, 1857

As the drama surrounding the Kansas-Nebraska compromise unfolded, events were also playing out in the United States Supreme Court which would push the country closer to war.

Dr. John Emerson, a U.S. Army surgeon, owned a slave named Dred Scott. Over the course of his army career, the doctor moved Scott from the slave state of Missouri to the free state of Illinois and then into the free territory of Wisconsin. While in Wisconsin, Scott married Harriett Robinson and her owner transferred her to Dr. Emerson.

After many years, the military ordered Emerson back to Missouri and he eventually died there. Scott sought to purchase the freedom of both himself and his wife from Emerson's widow but she declined the offer. Abolitionists then helped Scott file a lawsuit to declare his status as a free man because he had lived in free states and territories for so long. The case ended up in the United States Supreme Court after moving through lower courts over the course of nine years. Finally, in

March 1857, by a vote of 7-2, the Court ruled that no slave or descendant of a slave could be a U.S. citizen. Further, as a non-citizen, Scott had no rights to sue in court and must remain a slave. The Court completely ignored the long-standing precedent that black men in five of the original states had been treated as fully empowered citizens since the time of the Declaration of Independence.

As a further assault on the sentiments of the anti-slavery North, the Court also found that Congress could not prohibit slavery in the newly-emerging territories and declared the Missouri Compromise of 1820 to be unconstitutional.

The ruling was not a great surprise when the Court's makeup is considered. Five of the nine justices had been appointed by presidents with roots in the South. The Chief Justice, Roger Taney, was a firm supporter of slavery. The ruling, however, was extremely controversial and was another factor that prompted Abraham Lincoln to reenter politics.

"The question before us is, whether (people of African ancestry)...compose a portion of this people, and are constituent members of this sovereignty? We think they are not, and that they are not included, and were not intended to be included, under the word citizens in the Constitution, and can therefore claim none of the rights and privileges which that instrument provides for and secures to citizens of the United states."

— Chief Justice Roger B. Taney, writing for the
Supreme Court in Dred Scott v. Sandford, 1857

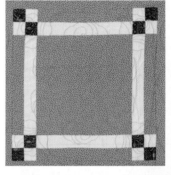

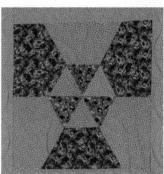

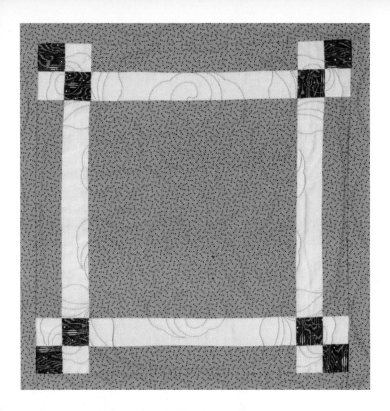

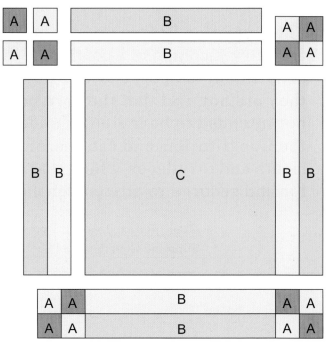

Block No. 23

FINISHED SIZE: 12″ SQUARE

FABRICS REQUIRED: TAN PRINT, BROWN PRINT, CHEDDAR PRINT
TEMPLATES ARE FOUND ON PAGES 91.

CUTTING

From the brown print, cut:
  8 – 1 1/2″ A squares.

From the tan print, cut:
  8 – 1 1/2″ A squares.
  4 – 1 1/2″ x 8 1/2″ B rectangles.

From the cheddar print, cut:
  4 – 1 1/2″ x 8 1/2″ B rectangles.
  1 – 8 1/2″ C square (no template given).

PIECING

Refer to diagram for placement.

FOUR-PATCH UNITS

1. Lay out 2 brown A squares and 2 tan squares. Sew into a four-patch unit. Make 4.

RECTANGLE UNITS

2. Sew 1 tan B rectangle to 1 cheddar B rectangle. Make 4.

ROWS

3. Sew 2 four-patch units to either side of 1 rectangle unit. Make 2.

4. Sew 2 rectangle units to either side of the cheddar C square.

BLOCK ASSEMBLY

5. Lay out the 3 rows and sew together as shown in the block diagram.

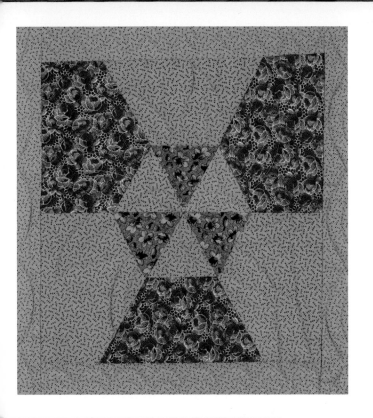

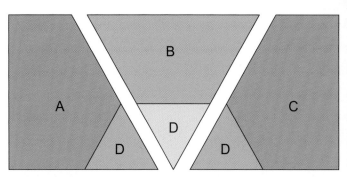

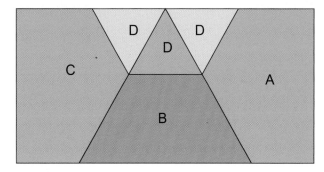

Block No. 24

FINISHED SIZE: 12″ SQUARE

FABRICS REQUIRED: BROWN PRINT NO. 1, BROWN PRINT NO. 2, CHEDDAR PRINT
TEMPLATES ARE FOUND ON PAGES 92-94.

CUTTING

From the brown print No. 1, cut:
  3 – D templates.

From the cheddar print, cut:
  1 – A template.
  1 – B template.
  1 – C template.
  3 – D templates.

From the brown print No. 2, cut:
  1 – A template.
  1 – B template.
  1 – C template.

PIECING

Refer to the diagram for placement.

1. Sew 3 brown print No. 1 D
templates to each of the cheddar A,
B and C templates.

2. Sew 3 cheddar D templates to each
of the brown print No. 2 A, B and
C templates.

BLOCK ASSEMBLY

3. Lay out the units and sew together
as shown in the block diagram.

LEAFY REEL

Block No. 25

FINISHED SIZE: 12″ SQUARE

FABRICS REQUIRED: TAN PRINT, AGED MUSLIN (BACKGROUND)
TEMPLATES ARE FOUND ON PAGE 94.

CUTTING

From the tan print, cut:
   16 – A template.

From the background fabric, cut:
   1 – 13 1/2″ square.

APPLIQUE

Referring to the photo for placement, appliqué the shapes to the background square. Use the appliqué method of your choice. Trim block to 12 1/2″ after sewing.

Note: Fold the background fabric in half and half again and lightly finger press to form registration marks to aid placement. When placing the applique shapes on the background, be careful not to place them in the seam allowance.

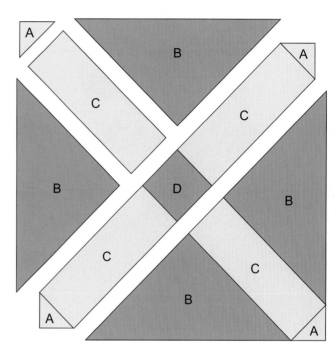

Block No. 26

FINISHED SIZE: 12″ SQUARE

FABRICS REQUIRED: TAN PRINT, BROWN PRINT
TEMPLATES ARE FOUND ON PAGE 95.

CUTTING

From the tan print, cut:
- 2 – 3 3/8″ squares. Cut on the diagonal to yield 4 A triangles.
- 4 – 2 5/8″ x 6 7/8″ C rectangles.

From the brown print, cut:
- 1 – 10 1/4″ square. Cut in half on both diagonals to yield 4 B triangles.
- 1 – 2 5/8″ D square.

PIECING

Refer to the diagram for placement.

1. Sew 2 brown B triangles to either side of 1 tan C rectangle. Sew 1 tan A triangle to the top of the tan C rectangle. Make 2.

2. Sew 2 tan C rectangles to either side of the brown D square. Sew 2 tan A triangles to both ends of this row. Make 1.

BLOCK ASSEMBLY

3. Lay out the 3 rows and sew together as shown in the block diagram.

CHAPTER 7

THE LINCOLN DOUGLAS DEBATES, 1858

A United States Senate race in Illinois became a pivotal battleground over the slavery question in 1858. The incumbent, Stephen Douglas, a Democrat, had been an active proponent of the Compromise of 1850. He advocated for popular sovereignty and sponsored the Kansas-Nebraska Act of 1854. Abraham Lincoln decided to challenge Douglas for the Senate seat because he opposed so many of Douglas' ideas. The relatively new Republican party welcomed Lincoln and the opportunity to take on Douglas.

Lincoln specifically believed that the United States could not function when it was divided between free states and slave-holding states. Both men were gifted speakers so the debates began drawing attention across the country. Newspapers covered the debates and stenographers transcribed the speeches so each man's thoughts were available for review and discussion. Ultimately, seven debates were held, one in each of the congressional districts in Illinois. The debate format allowed each speaker to fully outline his position. The first speaker talked for 60 minutes; the second speaker spoke for 90 minutes; then, the first speaker finished with a 30 minute response. The men alternated who started each event so they had opportunities to respond to points the other had made.

The second debate held in Freeport, Illinois, drew 15,000 people, significant because less than 5,000 people lived in the town at the time. Douglas worked to frame Lincoln as someone who wanted racial and social equality among the races, a theme which tended to scare poorer white citizens who were worried about their own economic well-being. Lincoln, in contrast, argued that he simply wanted to avoid adding more slave-holding states or territories to the Union, but he understood why some areas were dependent on slavery. He acknowledged that while he generally wanted to abolish slavery, doing so would take time and work especially in the South where the economy was so dependent upon the labor.

Douglas then set forth the Freeport Doctrine, his attempt to satisfy both those for and against slavery. Basically a restatement of the concept of popular sovereignty, the doctrine provided that the people actually living in any new territory should have the ability to decide whether their area allowed slavery. The position ended up pleasing neither side. Southerners viewed it as a veiled attempt to abolish slavery, those in the North disliked the fact that slavery might continue in new areas.

At the time, state legislatures selected United States senators. The Illinois legislature was controlled by Democrats who selected Douglas as the winner. Although Lincoln lost the Senate election, the debate process defined him as a leader and in 1860 he would run for president.

"No man is good enough to govern another man without that other's consent."

— Abraham Lincoln at the debate.

"I believe this Government was made on the white basis. I believe it was made by white men for the benefit of white men and their posterity forever, and I am in favor of confining citizenship to white men, men of European birth and descent."

— Stephen Douglas at the debate.

QUADRILLE

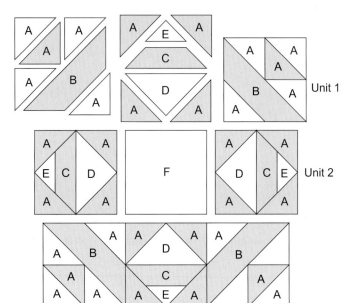

Unit 1

Unit 2

Block No. 27   **FINISHED SIZE: 12″ SQUARE**

FABRICS REQUIRED: TAN PRINT, LIGHT PRINT (BACKGROUND)
TEMPLATES ARE FOUND ON PAGES 96.

CUTTING

From the tan print, cut:
- 10 – 2 7/8″ squares. Cut each on the diagonal to yield 20 A triangles.
- 4 – B templates.
- 4 – C templates.

From the background, cut:
- 8 – 2 7/8″ squares. Cut each in half on the diagonal to yield 16 A triangles.
- 2 – 3 11/16″ squares. Cut each in half on the diagonal to yield 4 D triangles
- 1 – 4 1/2″ F square.
- 2 – 2 1/4″ squares. Cut each in half on the diagonal to yield 4 E triangles.

PIECING

This block contains two units – Unit 1 and Unit 2.

Refer to the diagram for placement.

UNIT 1

1. Sew 1 tan A triangle to 1 background A triangle. Make 4 half-square triangle units.
2. Sew 2 background A triangles to the sides of 1 half-square triangle. Make 4.
3. Sew 1 background A triangle to the short side of 1 tan B strip. Make 4.
4. Sew both sections together. Make 4.

UNIT 2

5. Sew 2 tan A triangles to either side of 1 background D triangle. Make 4 flying geese units.
6. Sew 1 background E triangle to the short side of 1 tan C strip. Make 4.
7. Sew 2 tan A triangles to either side of this unit. Make 4.
8. Sew both sections together. Make 4.

ROWS

9. Sew 2 Unit 1 to either side of 1 Unit 2. Make 2.
10. Sew 2 Unit 2 to either side of the F square. Make 1.

BLOCK ASSEMBLY

11. Lay out the 3 rows and sew together as shown in the block diagram

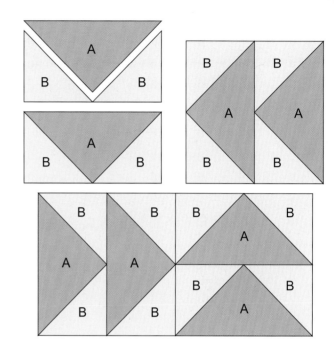

Block No. 28

FINISHED SIZE: 12″ SQUARE

FABRICS REQUIRED: BLUE PRINT, LIGHT PRINT (BACKGROUND)
TEMPLATES ARE FOUND ON PAGE 97.

CUTTING

From the blue print, cut:
- 2 – 7 1/4″ squares. Cut on both diagonals to yield 8 A triangles.

From the background, cut:
- 8 – 3 7/8″ squares. Cut each in half on the diagonal to yield 16 B triangles.

PIECING

Refer to the diagram for placement.
FLYING GEESE UNITS

1. Sew 2 background B triangles to 1 blue A triangle. Make 8.
2. Sew 2 flying geese units together. Make 4.

BLOCK ASSEMBLY

3. Lay out the 4 units and sew together as shown in the block diagram.

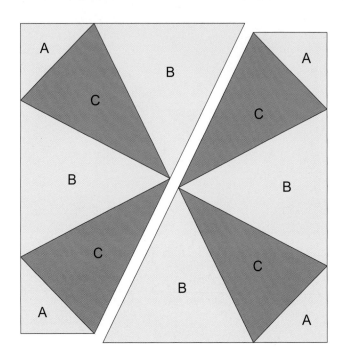

Block No. 29

FINISHED SIZE: 12˝ SQUARE

FABRICS REQUIRED: RED PRINT, CHEDDAR PRINT
TEMPLATES ARE FOUND ON PAGE 98.

CUTTING

From the red print, cut:
  4 – C templates.

From the cheddar print, cut:
  4 – A templates.
  4 – B templates.

PIECING

Refer to the diagram for placement.

1. Sew 2 red C triangles alternating with 2 cheddar B triangles. Make 2.

2. Sew 4 cheddar A triangles to the 4 red C triangles.

BLOCK ASSEMBLY

3. Lay out the 2 units and sew together as shown in the block diagram.

NINE PATCH CHECKERBOARD

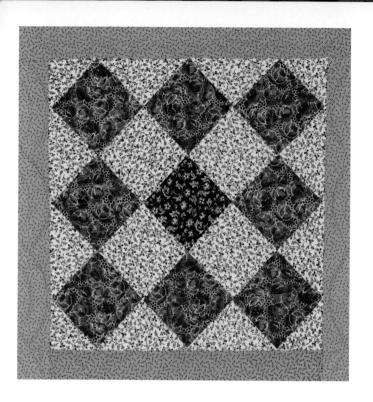

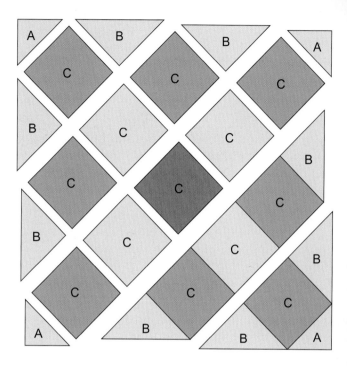

FINISHED SIZE: 12″ SQUARE

FABRICS REQUIRED: BROWN PRINT, BLACK PRINT, LIGHT PRINT (BACKGROUND)
TEMPLATES ARE FOUND ON PAGE 99.

CUTTING

From the brown print, cut:
  8 – 3 5/16″ C squares.

From the black print, cut:
  1 – 3 5/16″ C square.

From the background, cut:
  2 – 2 7/8″ squares. Cut each in half
    on the diagonal to yield 4 A
    triangles.
  2 – 5 1/4″ squares. Cut on both
    diagonals to yield 8 B triangles.
  4 – 3 5/16″ C squares.

PIECING

Rows

Note: It is helpful to sew this block
with a scant 1/4" seam allowance.

1. Sew 2 background B triangles to
   either side of 1 brown C square.
   Sew 1 background A triangle to
   the top. Make 2.
2. Sew 2 brown C squares to either
   side of 1 background C square. Sew
   2 background B triangles to either
   side. Make 2.
3. Sew 2 background C squares to
   either side of 1 black C square.
   Sew 2 brown C squares to either
   side of this. Sew 2 background A
   triangles to each end. Make 1.

BLOCK ASSEMBLY

4. Lay out the rows and sew together
   as shown in the block diagram.

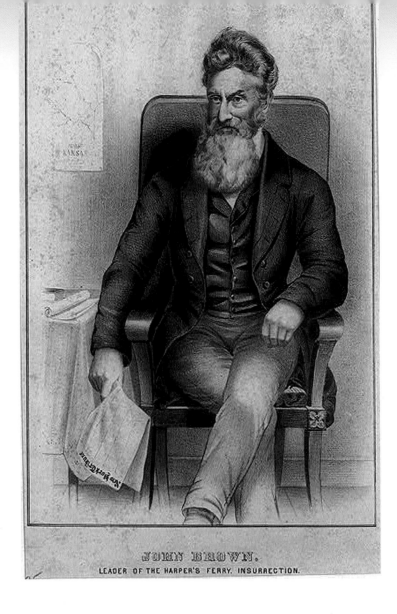

JOHN BROWN.
LEADER OF THE HARPER'S FERRY INSURRECTION.

CHAPTER 8

JOHN BROWN'S RAID, 1859

Born in 1800, John Brown spent his childhood in Ohio. Raised by a father who was adamantly against slavery, Brown adopted his father's views and began working for anti-slavery causes as a young man.

Brown lived in Kansas during the 1850s and was part of the violent response to the Kansas-Nebraska Act leading raids throughout Kansas and Missouri against slavery supporters. By 1859, Brown had decided the best way to stop slavery was to arm black men so they could rise up against their owners and start a war. With this in mind, he traveled back to Virginia and began plotting.

"I, John Brown, am quite certain that the crimes of this guilty land will never be purged away but with blood. I had, as I now think vainly, flattered myself that without very much bloodshed it might be done."

— John Brown, recorded on the day of his death, December 2, 1859.

Brown soon concluded that he could best start a conflict by raiding the federal arsenal located at Harper's Ferry, Virginia. He would distribute the weapons there to black men and encourage them to lead a revolt into the South. Brown organized several of his sons and neighbors and ultimately led an attack on the arsenal on October 16, 1859, with 16 white men and five black men.

Brown's followers held 60 of the town's prominent citizens hostage as part of their attack. Brown hoped by capturing the white men, slaves in the area would be encouraged to take up arms against their owners. Brown's men, however, were unorganized and fell within 36 hours to a counter-attack led by Robert E. Lee. Though wounded, Brown survived the attack and was charged with treason. Prior to being sentenced to death, Brown addressed the court:

" . . . I believe to have interfered as I have done . . . in behalf of His despised poor, was not wrong, but right. Now, if it be deemed necessary that I should forfeit my life for the furtherance of the ends of justice, and mingle my blood further with the blood of my children, and with the blood of millions in this slave country whose rights are disregarded by wicked, cruel, and unjust enactments, I submit: so let it be done."

While many in the North did not agree with Brown's tactics, his impassioned speech won him new respect among abolitionists. No one could question that Brown was willing to give his life for the ideals he embraced.

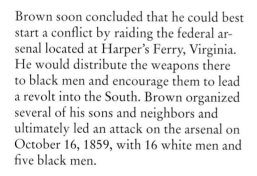

ROLLING STONE

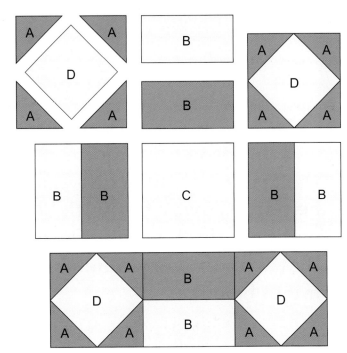

FINISHED SIZE: 12″ SQUARE

FABRICS REQUIRED: RED PRINT, LIGHT PRINT (BACKGROUND)
TEMPLATES ARE FOUND ON PAGE 100.

CUTTING

From the red print, cut:
- 8 – 2 7/8″ squares. Cut each in half on the diagonal to yield 16 A triangles.
- 4 – 2 1/2″ x 4 1/2″ B rectangles.

From the background, cut:
- 4 – 2 1/2″ x 4 1/2″ B rectangles.
- 1 – 4 1/2″ C square.
- 4 – 3 5/16″ D squares.

PIECING

Refer to the diagram for placement.

SQUARE-IN-A-SQUARE UNITS

1. Sew 4 A triangles to the sides of 1 background D square. Make 4.

RECTANGLE UNITS

2. Sew 1 background B rectangle to 1 red B rectangle. Make 4.

ROWS

3. Sew 2 square-in-a-square units to either side of 1 rectangle unit. Make 2.

4. Sew 2 rectangle units to either side of 1 background C square. Make 1.

BLOCK ASSEMBLY

5. Lay out the rows and sew together as shown in the block diagram.

BARRISTER'S BLOCK

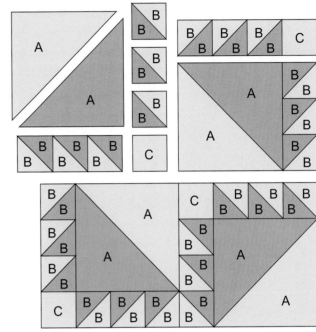

Block No. 32

FINISHED SIZE: 12″ SQUARE

FABRICS REQUIRED: PINK PRINT, BLUE PRINT
TEMPLATES ARE FOUND ON PAGE 101.

CUTTING

From the pink print, cut:
- 2 – 5 3/8″ squares. Cut each in half on the diagonal to yield 4 A triangles.
- 12 – 2 3/8″ squares. Cut each in half on the diagonal to yield 24 B triangles.
- 4 – 2″ C squares.

From the blue print, cut:
- 2 – 5 3/8″ squares. Cut each in half on the diagonal to yield 4 A triangles.
- 12 – 2 3/8″ squares. Cut each in half on the diagonal to yield 24 B triangles.

PIECING

Refer to the diagram for placement.

HALF-SQUARE TRIANGLE UNITS

1. Sew 1 pink B triangle to 1 blue B triangle. Make 24 small units.
2. Sew 1 pink A triangle to 1 blue A triangle. Make 4 large units.
3. Sew 3 small half-square units together. Make 4. Make sure all the triangles are going in the same direction.
4. Sew 3 half-square units together, making sure the triangles are the mirror image of the Step 3 triangles. Sew 1 pink C square to the end of these units. Make 4.

5. Sew 1 Step 3 Unit to 1 large half-square triangle unit. Make 4.
6. Sew 1 Step 4 Unit to the adjacent side. Make 4.

BLOCK ASSEMBLY

7. Lay out the 4 units and sew together as shown in the block diagram.

RED CROSS

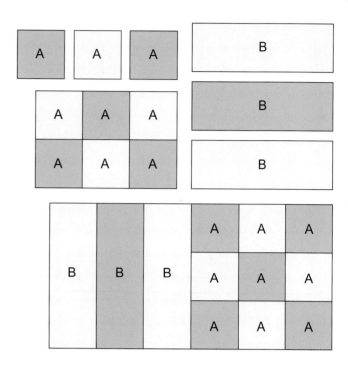

FINISHED SIZE: 12″ SQUARE

FABRICS REQUIRED: PINK PRINT, LIGHT PRINT (BACKGROUND)
TEMPLATES ARE FOUND ON PAGE 101.

CUTTING

From the pink print, cut:
- 10 – 2 1/2″ A squares.
- 2 – 2 1/2″ x 6 1/2″ B rectangles.

From the background, cut:
- 8 – 2 1/2″ A squares.
- 4 – 2 1/2″ x 6 1/2″ B rectangles.

PIECING

NINE-PATCH UNITS

1. Sew 5 pink A squares and 4 background A squares into a nine-patch unit. Make 2.

RAIL UNITS

2. Sew 2 background B rectangles to either side of 1 pink B rectangle. Make 2.

BLOCK ASSEMBLY

3. Lay out the 4 units and sew together as shown in the block diagram.

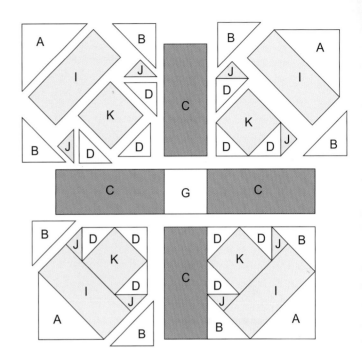

Block No. 34 FINISHED SIZE: 12˝ SQUARE

FABRICS REQUIRED: LIGHT TAN PRINT, BROWN PRINT, LIGHT PRINT (BACKGROUND)
TEMPLATES ARE FOUND ON PAGE 102.

CUTTING

From the brown print, cut:
4 –2 1/2˝ x 5 1/2˝ C rectangles.

From the light tan print, cut:
4 – 2 1/4˝ x 4 3/4˝ I rectangles.
2 – 2 3/4˝ squares. Cut on both diagonal to yield 8 J triangles.
4 – 2 5/8˝ K squares.

From the background, cut:
2 – 3 7/8˝ squares. Cut each in half on the diagonal to yield 4 A triangles.
4 – 2 7/8˝ squares. Cut each in half on the diagonal to yield 8 B triangles.
6 – 2 3/8˝ squares. Cut each in half on the diagonal to yield 12 D triangles.
1 – 2 1/2˝ G square.

PIECING

Refer to the diagram for placement.

"T" UNITS

1. Sew 1 J tan triangle to 1 background D triangle. Make 4.
2. Sew 1 J tan triangle to 1 background D triangle, making sure this is the mirror image of the Step 1 units. Make 4. Sew these units to either side of 1 tan K square. Sew 1 background D triangle to the bottom. Make 4.
3. Sew 1 tan I rectangle to the top of this unit. Sew 1 background A triangle to the tan I rectangle. Make 4.
4. Sew 2 background B squares to either side of this unit, making sure the long side touches the tan I rectangle and tan J triangle. Make 4.

Rows

7. Sew 2 "T" units to either side of 1 brown C rectangle. Make 2.
8. Sew 2 brown C rectangles to either side of 1 background G square. Make 1.

BLOCK ASSEMBLY

9. Lay out the rows and sew together as shown in the block diagram.

CHAPTER 9

THE ELECTION OF 1860

By 1860, most Americans had an opinion on the slave issue and whether newly added states should be deemed free or slaveholding. The various attempts at compromise over the years had only solidified opinions and strengthened the resolve of those on both sides of the slavery question rather than actually achieving any workable middle ground. Thus, the presidential election of 1860 became a critical test as to how the country would ultimately resolve the issue.

During the early days of the Union, the two-party political system successfully operated with both the Whig Party and the Democratic Party being fairly evenly represented in state and national offices. By the 1850s, the Whig Party was in disarray, effectively split apart over the slavery issue. The Democratic Party, more prominent in the South managed to stay together but the issue weakened it as well.

Out of this chaos, a new party, the Republican Party, emerged in the North. Making opposition to slavery its key position, the Republican Party quickly grew in numbers by promoting a moderate approach on the question of slavery. The party acknowledged that

states, particularly those in the South, should have the right to determine their own laws on slavery. These moderates supported the Fugitive Slave Act and accepted its enforcement. Unlike true abolitionists, the moderate Republicans were willing to tolerate slavery while slowly pushing for changes that would give more slaves the opportunity for freedom.

In May 1860, Republicans gathered to nominate a candidate for President. Their platform advocated that territories in the country should normally be considered "free" but did not demand an end to slavery at once. After much discussion, Abraham Lincoln emerged as the Republican candidate.

When the Democrats gathered to select a candidate in April 1860, the slavery issue threatened to splinter the party. Northern Democrats generally supported the popular sovereignty concept thinking that most new states would opt against slavery. Southern Democrats realized that the sovereignty concept alone would not guarantee that new states have slave-holding rights. Therefore, they promoted the idea of a mandate for slavery in all remaining territories. The two sides could

"A house divided against itself cannot stand. I believe this government cannot endure permanently half slave and half free. I do not expect the Union to be dissolved; I do not expect the house to fall; but I do expect that it will cease to be divided. It will become all the one thing or all the other. Either the opponents of slavery will arrest the further spread of it and place it where the public mind shall rest in the belief that it is in course of ultimate extinction, or its advocates will push it forward until it shall become alike lawful in all the states, old as well as new, north as well as south."

— Abraham Lincoln, June 16, 1858, Address to the Republican Convention

not agree and many Southern Democrats walked out of the convention so the party was unable to nominate a candidate.

By June 1860, the two factions of the Democratic Party realized they could not reach a compromise. So, the party met in two separate conventions and nominated two different candidates. The northern wing nominated Stephen Douglas, well-known for his attempts to work out compromises in the past. The southern wing nominated John Breckenridge who embraced the concept that the federal government should ensure the right to hold slaves in all remaining territories.

To further add to the confusion, a fourth political party emerged in 1860. Composed primarily of conservatives who were not happy that the other parties were promoting regional issues, the Constitutional Party advocated a strong, united country that ignored differences among the North and South. The Constitutional Party nominated John Bell as its presidential candidate. The party found support in the border states who were caught in the middle of the debate.

As the election unfolded, the extent of the breakdown of a national government became apparent. Many southern states refused to list Lincoln on their ballot. By the time of the election, the race had divided into two separate contests. In the north, Lincoln battled Douglas for votes. In the South, Breckenridge battled Bell. Supporters of both men hinted that if their candidate did not win, then southern states would secede from the Union.

Ultimately, Lincoln won the popular vote in the north carrying 17 states. Breckenridge carried 11 southern states. Thus, Lincoln won the election, but when vote totals were tabulated among the four candidates, he had only a plurality of the total votes, not a clear majority.

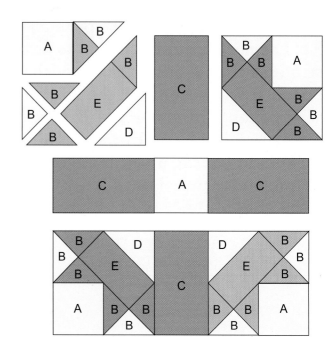

FINISHED SIZE: 12″ SQUARE

FABRICS REQUIRED: BROWN PRINT, RED PRINT, LIGHT PRINT (BACKGROUND)
TEMPLATES ARE FOUND ON PAGE 103.

CUTTING

From the brown print, cut:
 2 – 3 5/8″ squares. Cut on both diagonals to yield 8 B triangles.
 2 – 2 3/16″ x 3 7/8″ E rectangles.

From the red print, cut:
 2 – 3 5/8″ squares. Cut on both diagonals to yield 8 B triangles.
 4 – 2 7/8″ x 5 5/16″ C rectangles.
 2 – 2 3/16″ x 3 7/8″ E rectangles.

From the background, cut:
 5 – 2 7/8″ A squares.
 2 – 3 5/8″ squares. Cut on both diagonals to yield 8 B triangles.

 2 – 3 1/4″ squares. Cut each in half on the diagonal to yield 4 D triangles.

PIECING

Refer to the diagram for placement.

1. Sew the short side 1 brown B triangle to the short side of 1 background B triangle. Make 2.
2. Sew 2 of these units to either side of 1 background A square. Make 2.
3. Sew 2 brown B triangles to either side of 1 brown E rectangle. Sew 1 background D triangle to the bottom. Make 2.

4. Sew both units together to form a square. Make 2 brown units.
5. Repeat with the red units. Make 2 red units.

Rows

6. Sew 1 brown unit and 1 red unit to either side of 1 red C rectangle. Make 2.
7. Sew 2 red C rectangles to either side of 1 background A square. Make 1.

BLOCK ASSEMBLY

8. Lay out the rows and sew together as shown in the block diagram.

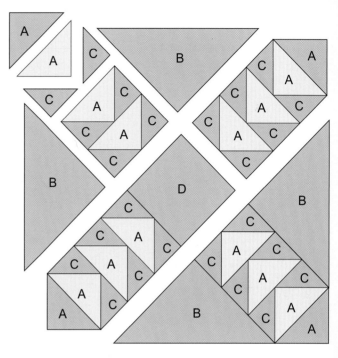

Block No.36

FINISHED SIZE: 12″ SQUARE

FABRIC REQUIRED: BLUE PRINT, LIGHT PRINT
TEMPLATES ARE FOUND ON PAGE 104.

CUTTING

From the light print, cut:
  6 – 3 1/4″ squares. Cut each in half on the diagonal to yield 12 A triangles.

From the blue print, cut:
  2 – 3 1/4″ squares. Cut each in half on the diagonal to yield 4 A triangles.
  1 – 8 3/4″ squares. Cut on both diagonals to yield 4 B triangles.
  12 – 3 5/8″ squares. Cut on both diagonals to yield 24 C triangles
  1 – 3 7/8 D square.

PIECING

Refer to diagram for placement.
FLYING GEESE UNITS

1. Sew 2 blue C triangles to either side of 1 light A triangle. Make 12.
2. Sew 3 flying geese units into a row.

ROWS

2. Sew 2 blue B triangles to either side of 1 set of 3 flying geese units. Sew 1 blue A triangle to the top. Make 2.
3. Sew 2 sets of 3 flying geese units to either side of 1 blue D square. Sew 2 blue A triangles to the ends. Make 1.

BLOCK ASSEMBLY

4. Lay out the rows and sew together as shown in the block diagram.

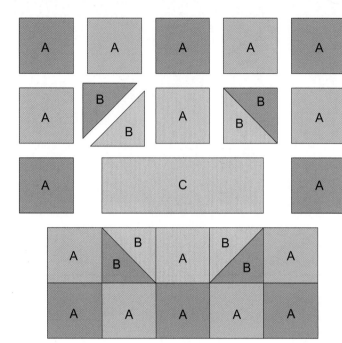

Block No. 37

FINISHED SIZE: 9″ SQUARE

FABRICS REQUIRED: RED PRINT, PINK PRINT, LIGHT PRINT
TEMPLATES ARE FOUND ON PAGE 105.

CUTTING

From the light print, cut:
  2 – 2 5/16″ A squares.
  2 – B templates.
  1 – 2 5/16″ x 5 7/8″ C rectangle.

From the red print, cut:
  8 – 2 5/16″ A squares.
  2 – B templates.

From the pink print, cut:
  8 – 2 5/16″ A squares.

PIECING

Refer to diagram for placement.

HALF-SQUARE TRIANGLE UNITS

1. Sew 1 light B triangle to 1 red B triangle. Make 4.

ROWS

2. Sew 2 pink squares alternating with 3 red A squares starting with the red in a row. Make 2.

3. Lay out 2 pink A squares, 2 half-square triangle unit and 1 light A square and sew together. Make 2.

4. Lay out 2 red A squares and 1 background C rectangle and sew together. Make 1.

BLOCK ASSEMBLY

5. Lay out the rows and sew together as shown in the block diagram.

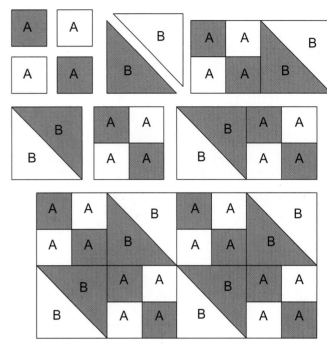

Block No. 39

FINISHED SIZE: 9″ SQUARE

**FABRICS REQUIRED: BROWN PRINT, LIGHT PRINT (BACKGROUND)
TEMPLATES ARE FOUND ON PAGE 105.**

CUTTING

From the brown print, cut:
- 16 – 1 5/8″ A squares.
- 4 – 3 1/8″ squares. Cut each in half on the diagonal to yield 8 B triangles.

From the background print, cut:
- 16 – 1 5/8″ A squares.
- 4 – 3 1/8″ squares. Cut each in half on the diagonal to yield 8 B triangles.

PIECING

Refer to diagram for placement.

FOUR-PATCH UNITS

1. Lay out 2 background A squares and 2 brown A squares. Sew into a four-patch unit. Make 8.

HALF-SQUARE TRIANGLE UNITS

2. Sew 1 background B triangle to 1 brown B triangle to make a half-square triangle unit. Make 8.

3. Sew 1 four-patch unit to 1 half-square triangle unit. Make 8.

4. Sew 2 of these units together. Make 4.

BLOCK ASSEMBLY

5. Lay out the 4 units and sew together as shown in the block diagram.

CHAPTER 10

DECLARATION OF THE CAUSES OF SECESSION, 1860

Following the election of Abraham Lincoln as President of the United States, Southerners worried that their way of life and economic well-being were under attack. While Lincoln's platform had not advocated an immediate end to slavery, southern leaders were convinced that he would outlaw slavery. Because their economy was so dependent on agriculture staffed by slaves, the entire way of life in the South was at risk.

South Carolina acted first drawing up a Declaration of Secession and leaving the Union on December 20, 1860. As part of its declaration, South Carolina created the Confederate States of America. Within four months, six more states seceded and joined the Confederacy. The additional states were: Alabama, Florida, Georgia, Louisiana, Mississippi and Texas. Then, Arkansas,

North Carolina, Tennessee and Virginia seceded and joined the Confederate States. The group elected Jefferson Davis to serve as their president.

President Lincoln refused to acknowledge the secessions. Many of the states had Army forts within their boundaries which were staffed by Union soldiers. Lincoln ordered these soldiers to stay at the forts. This action angered the secessionists. In many of the states, southern troops quickly ousted the Federal soldiers from the forts.

However, Fort Sumter remained under the control of U.S. government soldiers. Both sides considered Fort Sumter critical for their success—southerners argued that as long as federal troops controlled a key harbor port, the

Confederacy could not claim it was an independent nation. President Lincoln, inaugurated on March 6, 1861, vowed to reunite all states into one Union. Fort Sumter was an important symbol of the power of the United States government. As long as a Union flag flew in South Carolina, the state could not claim it had created its own government.

As the soldiers stayed under siege at Fort Sumter, their supplies dwindled. President Lincoln debated whether to withdraw the troops or take more aggressive action. Eventually, President Lincoln decided to separate the issue of providing supplies to starving men from the issue of providing additional troops to the fort. By sending in only relief supplies on unarmed ships, Lincoln hoped to put the South in a difficult position. If they turned back the supplies, they would be letting innocent men starve to death. If they fired on the relief ships, they would be the aggressors. Lincoln notified the southern leaders that the supplies were on the way and no military action would occur unless the South fired on the ships.

Leaders of the Confederacy met to discuss options. After much debate, the leaders decided to fire on and take Fort Sumter before the supplies arrived. Under the leadership of Brigadier General P.G.T. Beauregard, the South began firing. Fort Sumter stood for 33 hours before surrendering. During that

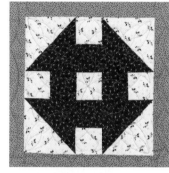

time, thousands of shots were fired. Remarkably, no one was killed or injured.

Following the surrender, Southerners celebrated that their quest for freedom had begun in earnest. Northerners were outraged at the military action. Depending on your perspective, the War Between the States, the Civil War or the War of Northern Aggression had begun on April 12, 1861.

During the next four years, more than 618,000 people would die as a result of the war. In an effort to end the war, General Sherman marched through the South and destroyed much of the southern infrastructure leaving the South's economy in shambles at the end of the war. As a result of the conflict, slavery ended, but the hostility and anger between those in the North and South remained. Through all of the conflict, the wives and mothers and other relatives of the soldiers remained at home with little access to information. Working on quilts such as the sampler featured in this book was an outlet and diversion from the controversy of the time.

SHOOFLY

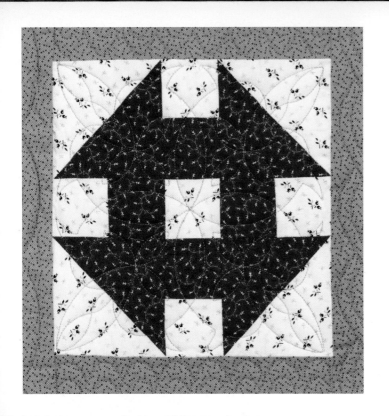

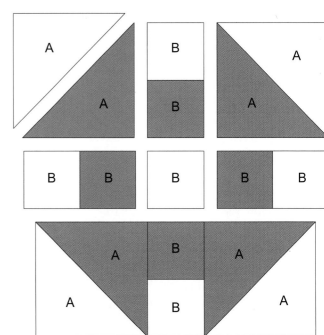

Block No. 40

FINISHED SIZE: 9″ SQUARE

FABRICS REQUIRED: RED PRINT, LIGHT PRINT (BACKGROUND)
TEMPLATES ARE FOUND ON PAGE 106.

CUTTING

From the red print, cut:
  2 – 4 1/2″ squares. Cut in half on the
    diagonal to yield 4 A triangles.
  4 – 2 5/16″ B squares.

From the background, cut:
  2 – 4 1/2″ squares. Cut in half on the
    diagonal to yield 4 A triangles.
  5 – 2 5/16″ B squares.

PIECING

Refer to the diagram for placement.
HALF-SQUARE TRIANGLE UNITS

1. Sew 1 red A triangle to 1 background A triangle to form a half-
   square triangle unit. Make 4.
2. Sew 1 red B square to 1 background
   B square. Make 4.

ROWS

3. Sew 2 half-square triangle units to
   either side of 1 Step 2 units.
   Make 2.
4. Sew 2 Step 2 units to either side of
   1 background B square. Make 1.

BLOCK ASSEMBLY

5. Lay out the rows and sew together
   as shown in the block diagram.

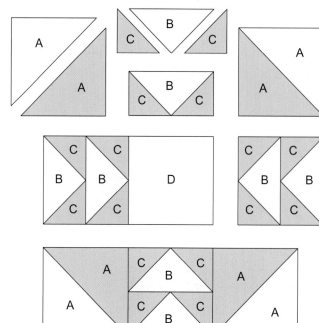

Block No. 41

FINISHED SIZE: 9″ SQUARE

FABRICS REQUIRED: GREEN PRINT, LIGHT PRINT (BACKGROUND)
TEMPLATES ARE FOUND ON PAGE 107.

CUTTING

Green Print:
- 2 – 3 7/8″ squares. Cut in half on the diagonal to yield 4 A triangles.
- 8 – 2 3/8″ squares. Cut in half on the diagonal to yield 16 C triangles.

Background:
- 2 – 3 7/8″ squares. Cut in half on the diagonal to yield 4 A triangles.
- 2 – 4 1/4″ squares. Cut on both diagonals to yield 8 B triangles.
- 1 – 2 3/8 square.

PIECING

Refer to the diagram for placement

HALF-SQUARE TRIANGLE UNITS

1. Sew 1 brown A triangle to 1 background A triangle unit to make a half-square triangle unit. Make 4.

FLYING GEESE UNITS

2. Sew 2 brown C triangles to either side of 1 background B triangle to make 1 flying geese unit. Make 8.
3. Sew two flying geese units together. Make 4.

ROWS

4. Sew 2 half-square triangle units to either side of a flying geese unit. Make 2.
5. Sew 2 flying geese units to either side of the background D square. Make 1.

BLOCK ASSEMBLY

6. Lay out the rows and sew together as shown in the block diagram.

SAWTOOTH

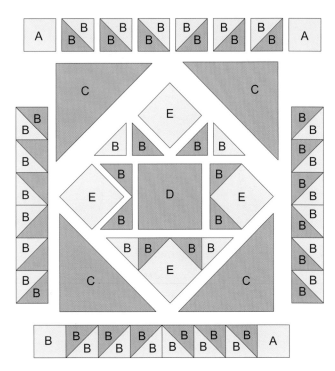

| **Block No. 43** | **FINISHED SIZE: 9″ SQUARE** |

FABRICS REQUIRED: BROWN PRINT, LIGHT PRINT (BACKGROUND)
TEMPLATES ARE FOUND ON PAGE 108.

CUTTING

From the blue print, cut:
- 16 – 2″ squares. Cut each in half on the diagonal to yield 32 B triangles.
- 2 – 4 1/4″ square. Cut each in half on the diagonal to yield 4 C triangles.
- 1 – 2 3/4″ D square.

From the background, cut:
- 4 – 1 5/8″ A squares.
- 14 – 2″ squares. Cut each in half on the diagonal to yield 28 B triangles.
- 4 – 2 1/16″ E squares.

PIECING

Refer to the diagram for placement.

MIDDLE STAR

1. Sew the short side 1 blue B triangle to the short side of 1 background B triangle. Make 4.
2. Sew 2 of these units to either side of 1 background E square. Make 2.
3. Sew 2 blue B triangles to adjacent sides of 1 background E square. Make 2.
4. Sew Step 2 units to either side of the blue D square. Make 1.
5. Sew the 3 units together in a row to make the Middle Star unit.
6. Sew 4 blue C squares to the sides of the Middle Star unit.

OUTER EDGES

7. Sew 1 blue B triangle to 1 background B triangle. Make 24.
8. Sew 3 half-square triangle units in a row with all the triangles going in one direction. Make 4.
9. Sew 3 half-square triangle units in a row with all the triangles going in the opposite direction of above. Make 4.
10. Sew 1 Step 8 unit to 1 Step 9 unit. Make 4.
11. Sew 2 A squares to the end of 1 of these units. Make 2.
12. Sew the 2 short half-square triangle rows to either side of the Middle Star.

BLOCK ASSEMBLY

13. Lay out the 3 rows and sew together as shown in the block diagram.

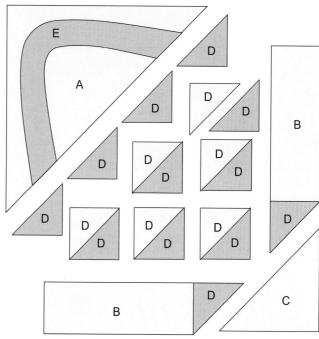

Block No. 44

FINISHED SIZE: 9″ SQUARE

**FABRICS REQUIRED: BROWN PRINT, LIGHT PRINT (BACKGROUND)
TEMPLATES ARE FOUND ON PAGE 109.**

CUTTING

From the brown print, cut:
- 6 – 2 11/16″ squares. Cut in half on the diagonal to yield 12 D triangles.
- 1 – E template.

From the background, cut:
- 1 – 8 1/16″ square. Cut in half on the diagonal to yield 1 A triangle. (Discard the extra triangle.)
- 2 – 2 5/16″ x 5 7/8″ B rectangles.
- 1 – 4 7/16″ square. Cut in half on the diagonal to yield 1 C triangle. (Discard the extra triangle.)
- 3 – 2 11/16″ squares. Cut in half on the diagonal to yield 6 D triangles.

PIECING

Refer to the diagram for placement.

HALF-SQUARE TRIANGLE UNITS

1. Sew 1 brown D triangle to 1 background D triangle to form a half-square triangle unit. Make 6.
2. Lay out the 6 half-square triangle units and 4 brown D triangles. Sew together to form the body of the basket.
3. Sew 1 brown D triangle to the end of 1 background B rectangle. Make 1.
4. Sew 1 brown D triangle to the end of 1 background B rectangle, making sure the brown D triangle is the mirror image of the Step 3 unit. Make 1.

5. Sew the Step 3 & 4 units to each side of the basket body.
6. Sew the background C triangle to the Step 5 unit .

APPLIQUE

7. Referring to the photo for placement, appliqué the brown E template (basket handle) to the background A triangle. Use the appliqué method of your choice.

BLOCK ASSEMBLY

8. Sew the A triangle and the basket together as shown in the block diagram.

TEMPLATES

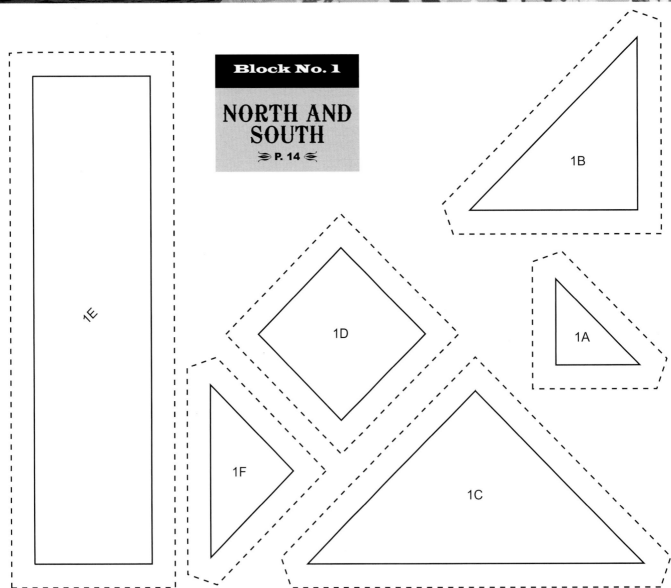

Block No. 1

NORTH AND SOUTH

≋ P. 14 ≋

1E

1B

1A

1D

1F

1C

2A

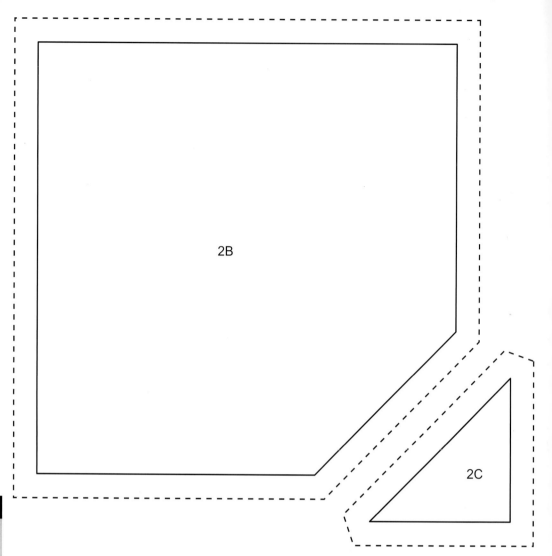

2B

2C

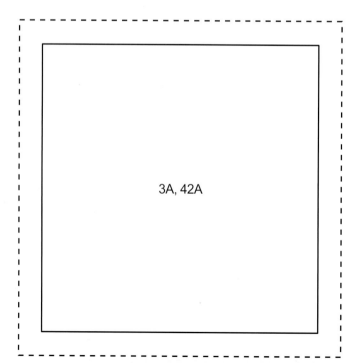

3A, 42A

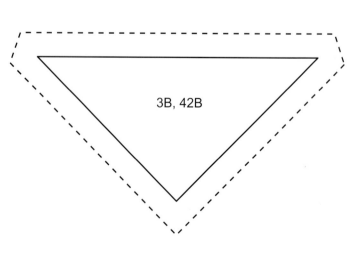

3B, 42B

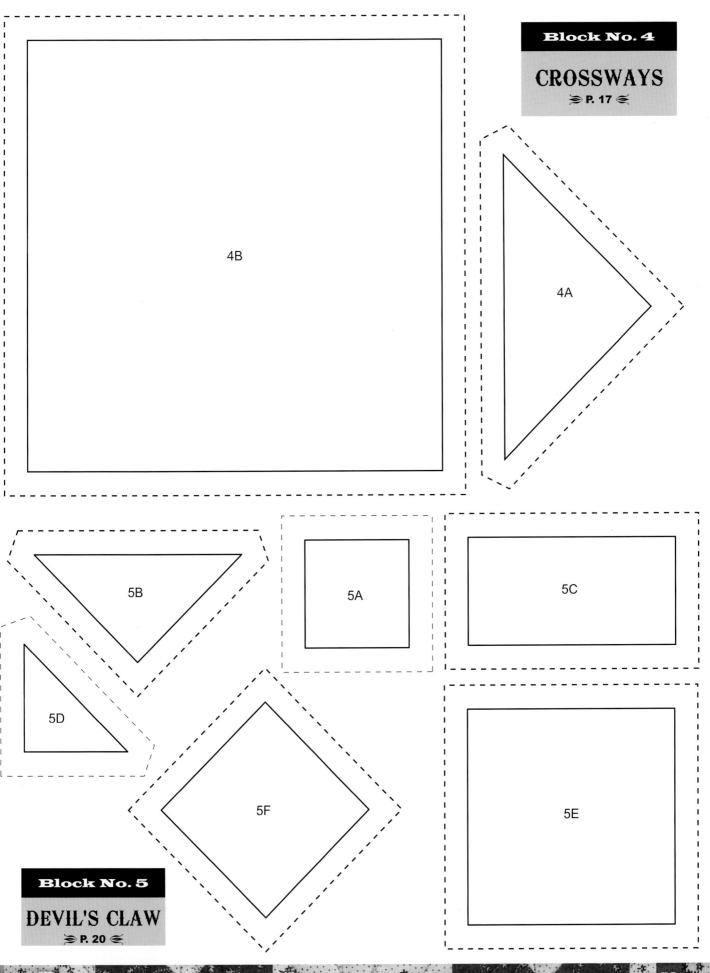

4B

4A

5B

5A

5C

5D

5F

5E

Block No. 5

DEVIL'S CLAW
P. 20

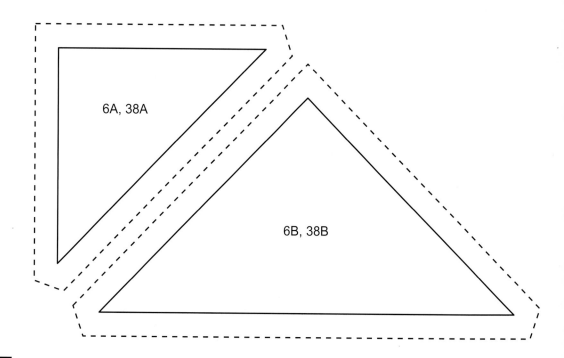

6A, 38A

6B, 38B

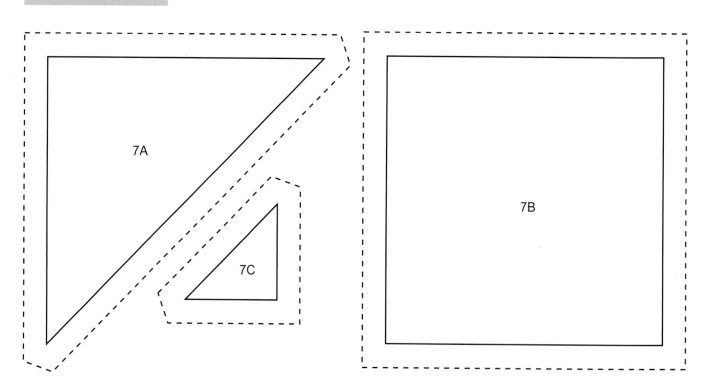

7A

7B

7C

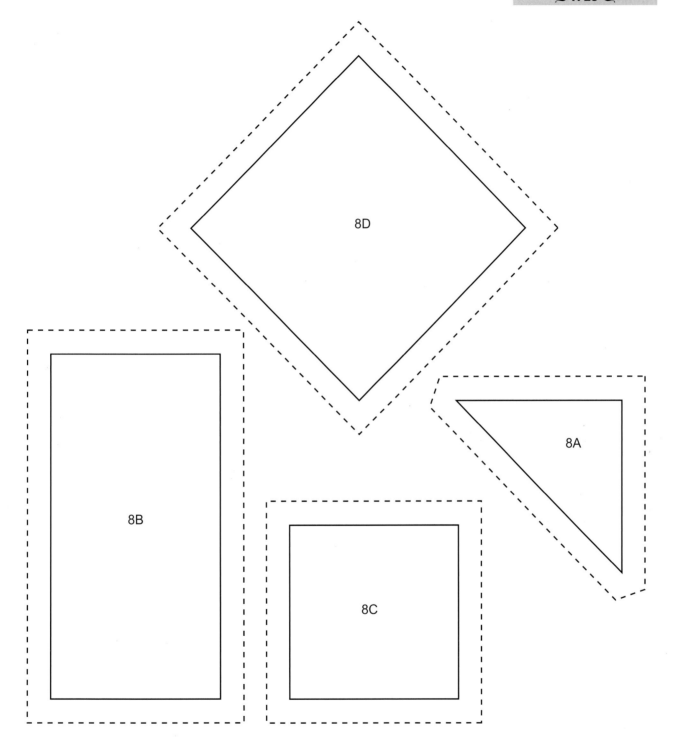

8D

8A

8B

8C

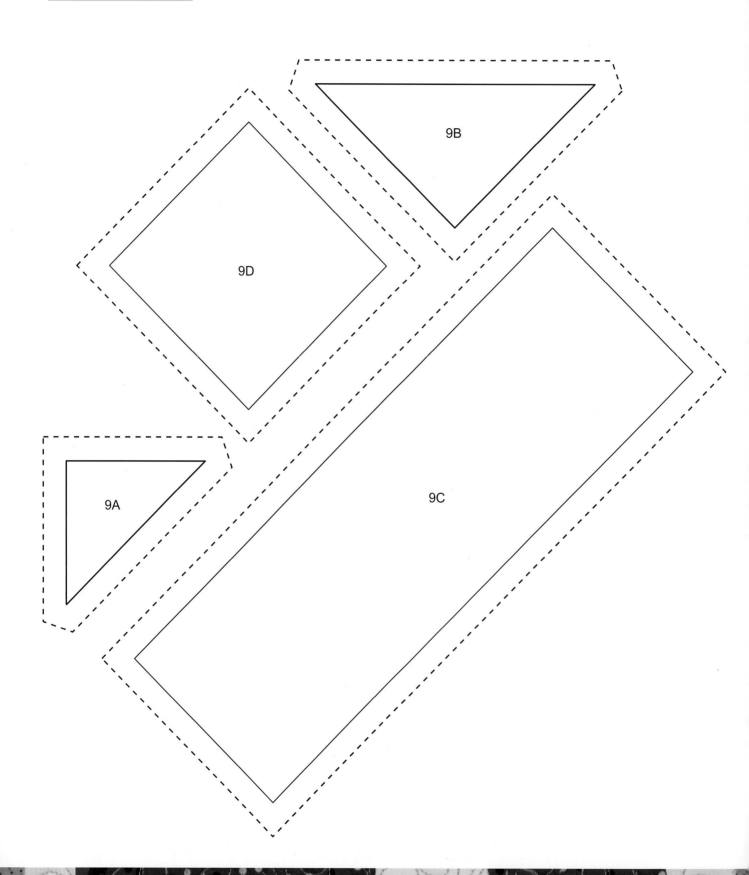

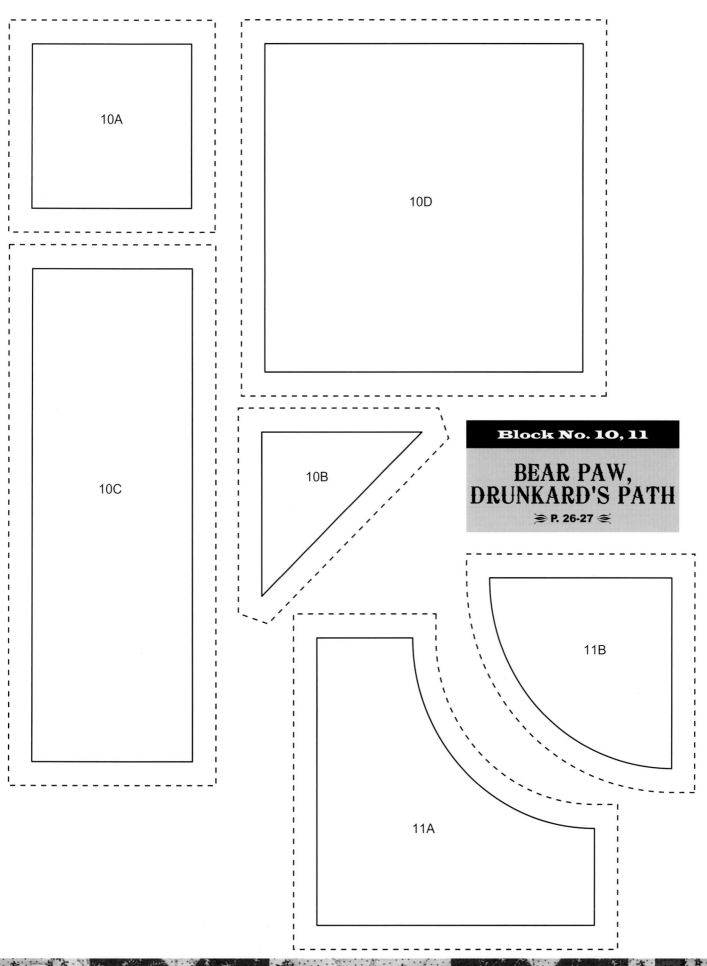

10A

10D

10C

10B

Block No. 10, 11

**BEAR PAW,
DRUNKARD'S PATH**

≥ P. 26-27 ≤

11B

11A

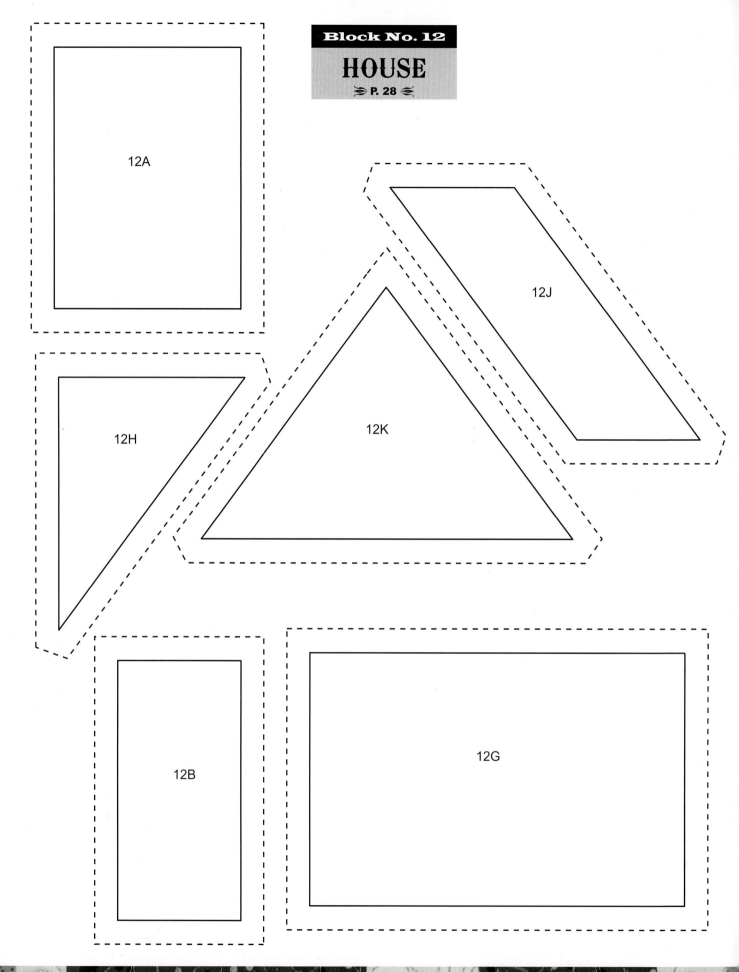

12A

12J

12H

12K

12B

12G

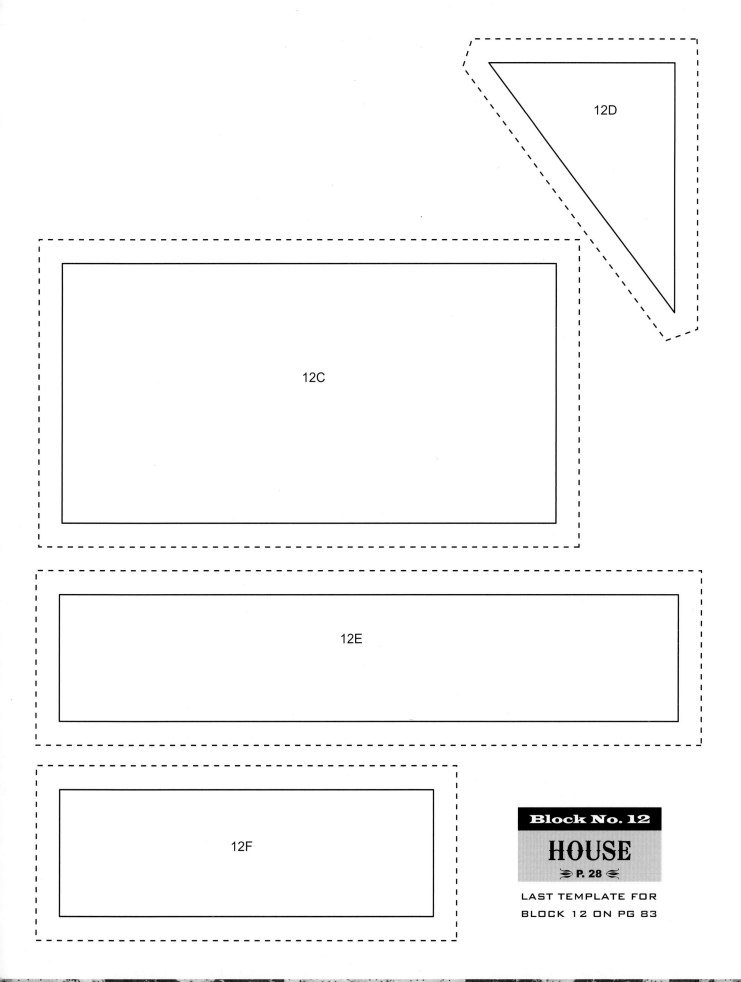

12D

12C

12E

Block No. 12

HOUSE

⇒ P. 28 ⇐

LAST TEMPLATE FOR
BLOCK 12 ON PG 83

12F

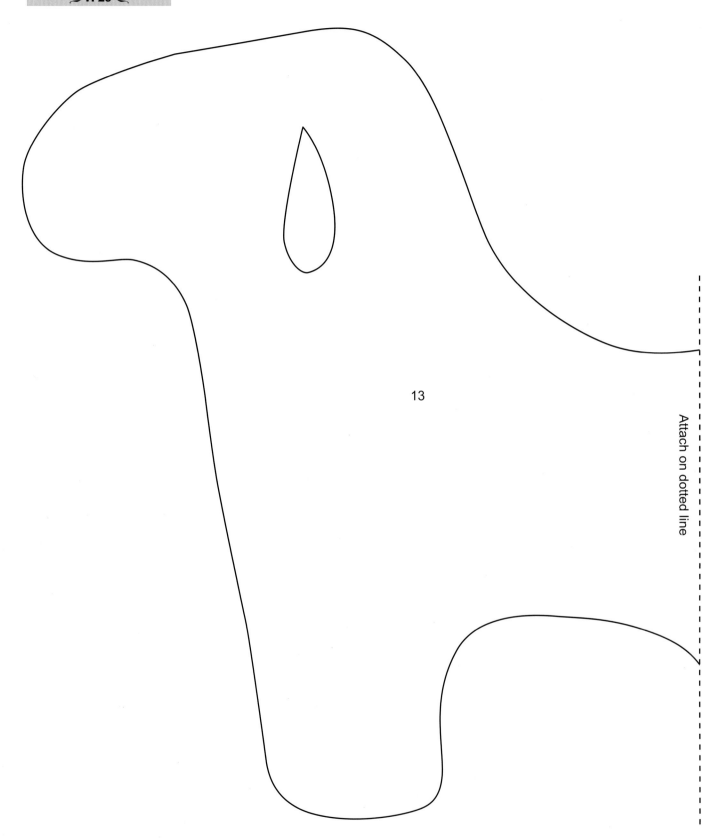

13

Attach on dotted line

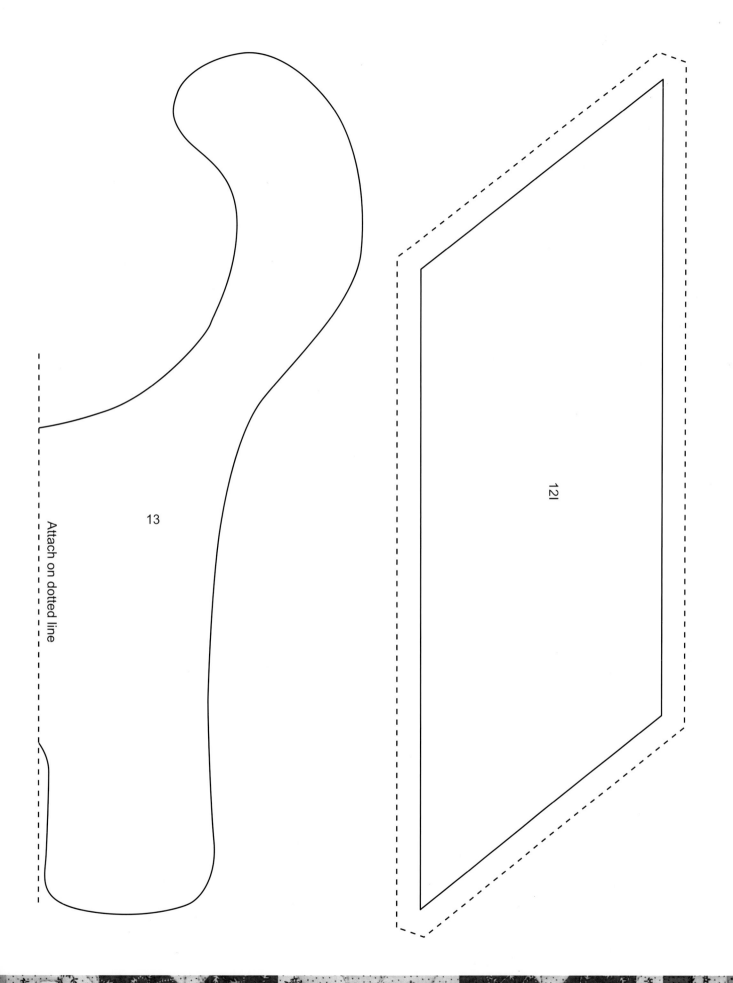

Attach on dotted line

13

12I

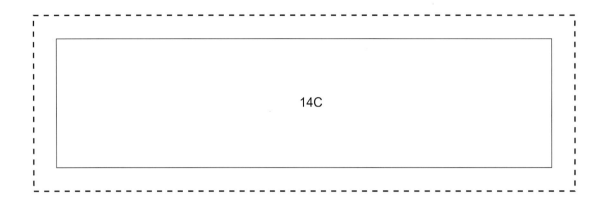

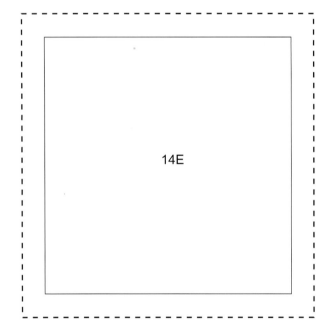

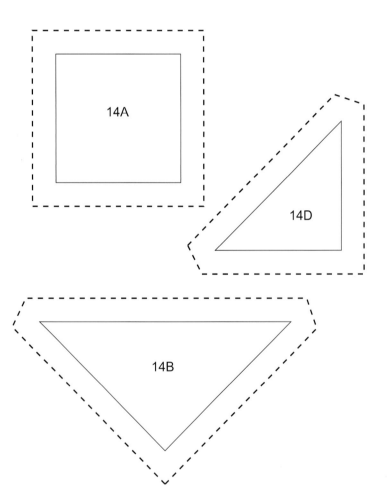

14C

14E

14A

14D

14B

Applique center
for Block 15

Template F

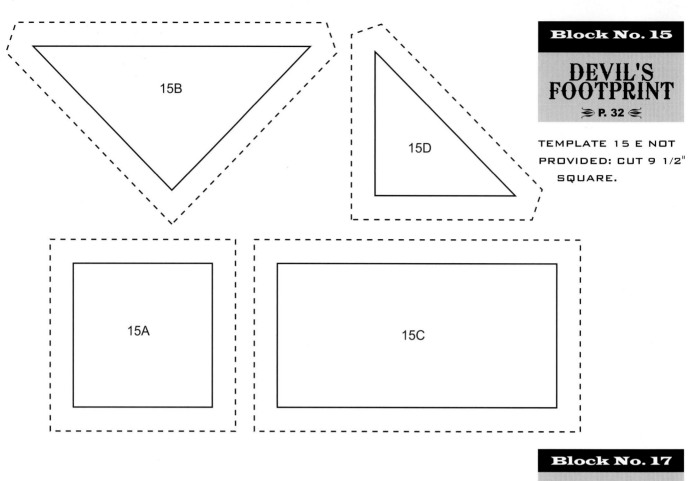

DEVIL'S FOOTPRINT

≥ P. 32 ≤

TEMPLATE 15 E NOT PROVIDED: CUT 9 1/2" SQUARE.

15B

15D

15A

15C

Block No. 17

MINI BOWS

≥ P. 34 ≤

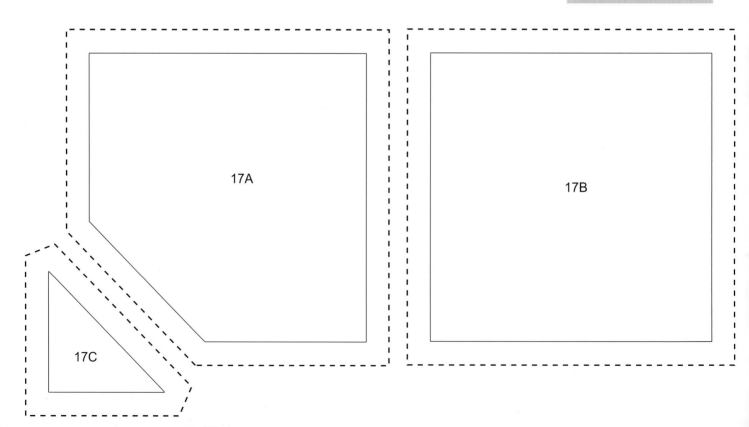

17A

17B

17C

Block No. 18

SKIRMISHES

P. 35

Attach on dotted line
18A
18B
18C
18C
Attach on dotted line

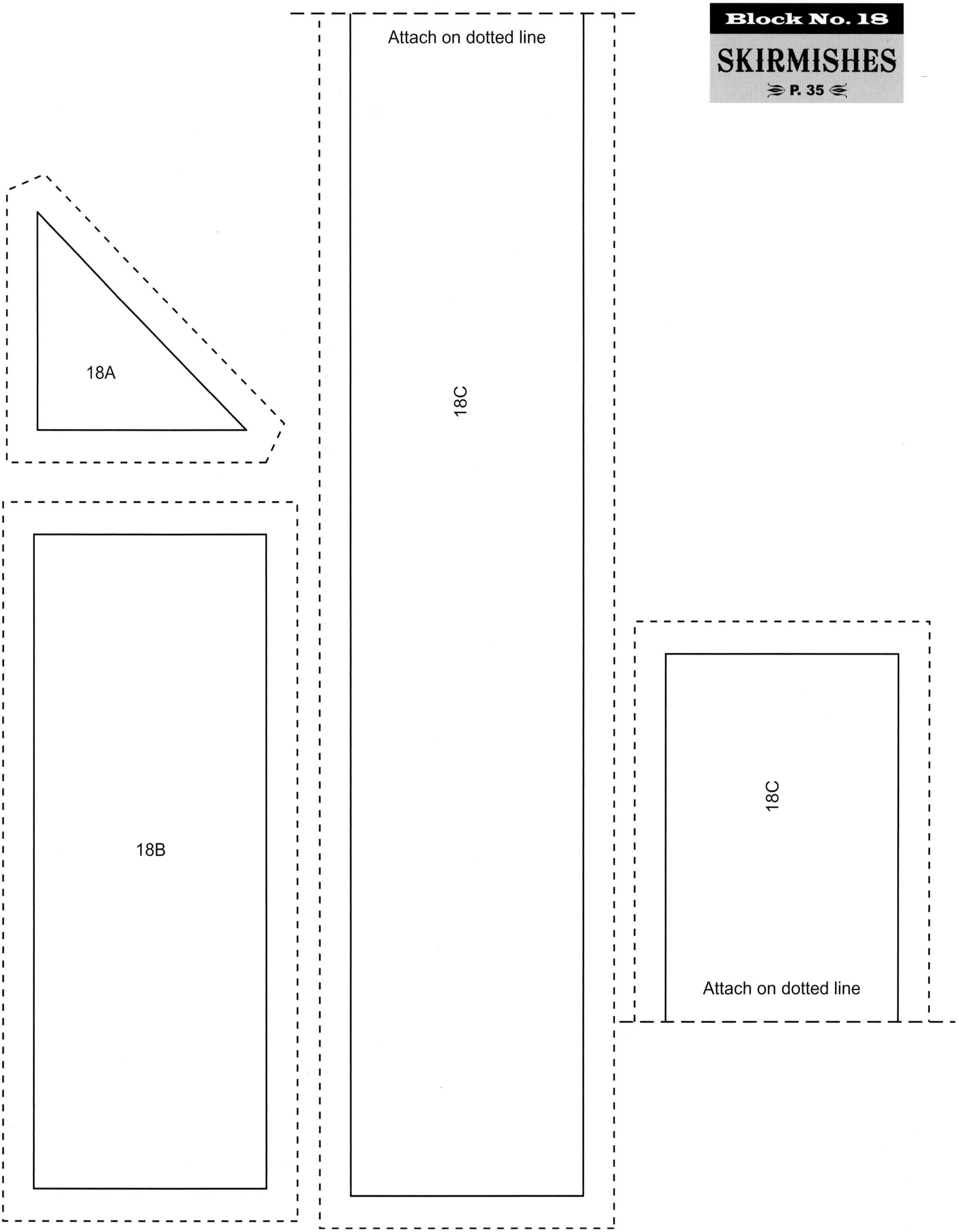

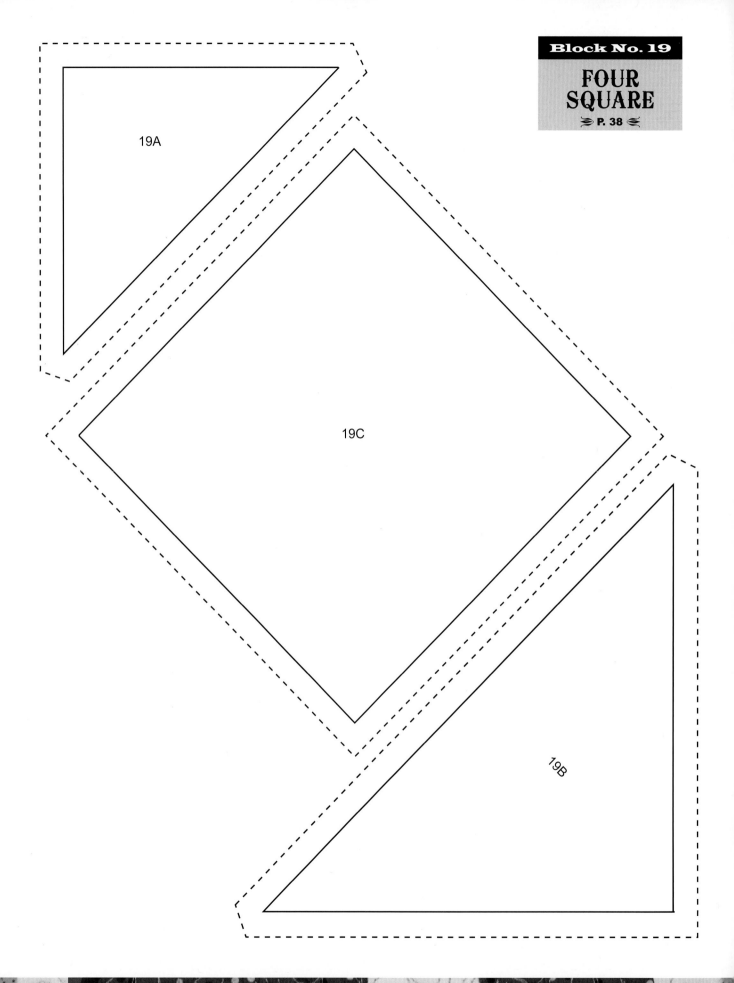

Block No. 19

FOUR SQUARE

≥ P. 38 ≤

19A

19C

19B

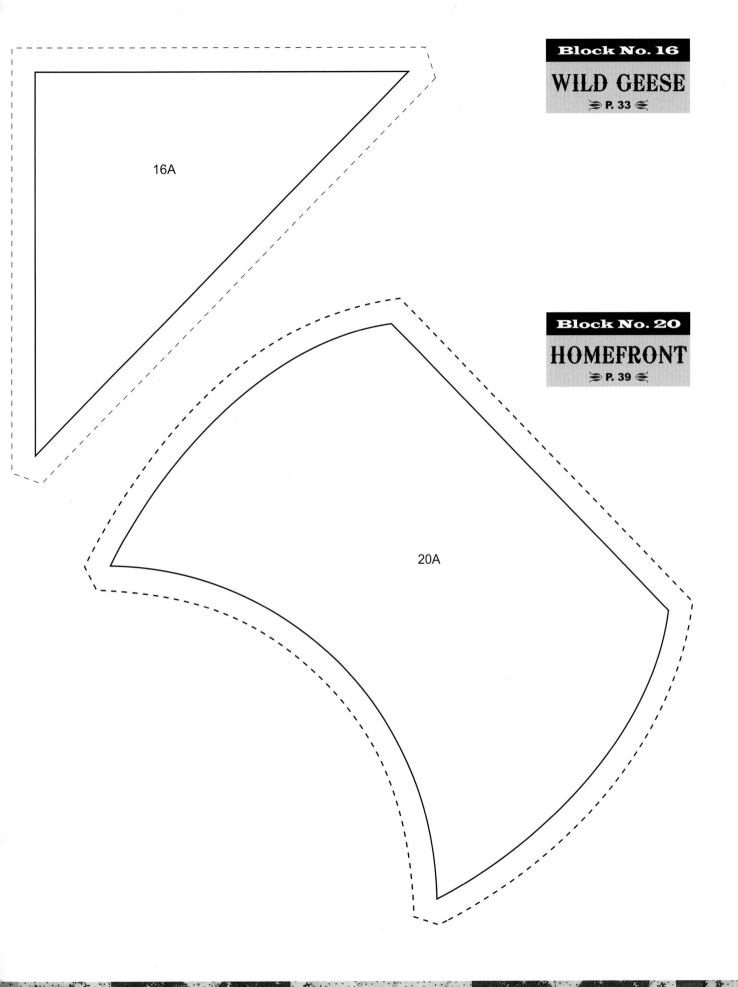

Block No. 16

WILD GEESE

≋ **P. 33** ≋

16A

Block No. 20

HOMEFRONT

≋ **P. 39** ≋

20A

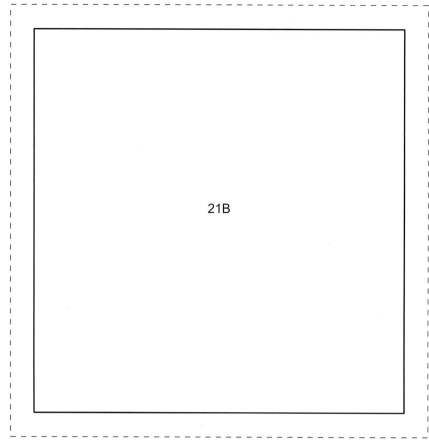

21B

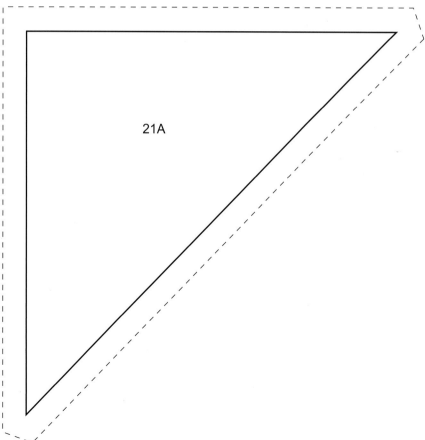

21A

TEMPLATE 23 C
NOT PROVIDED:
CUT 8 1/2" SQUARE.

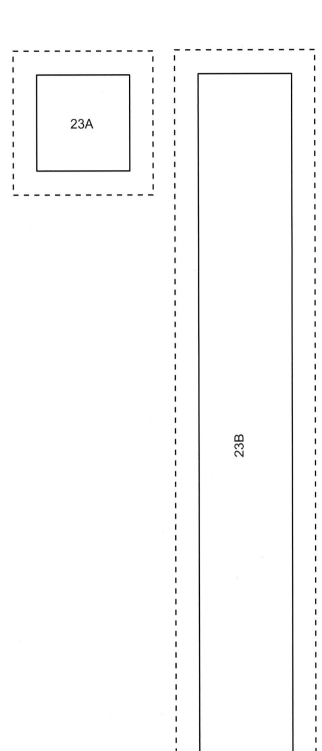

23A

23B

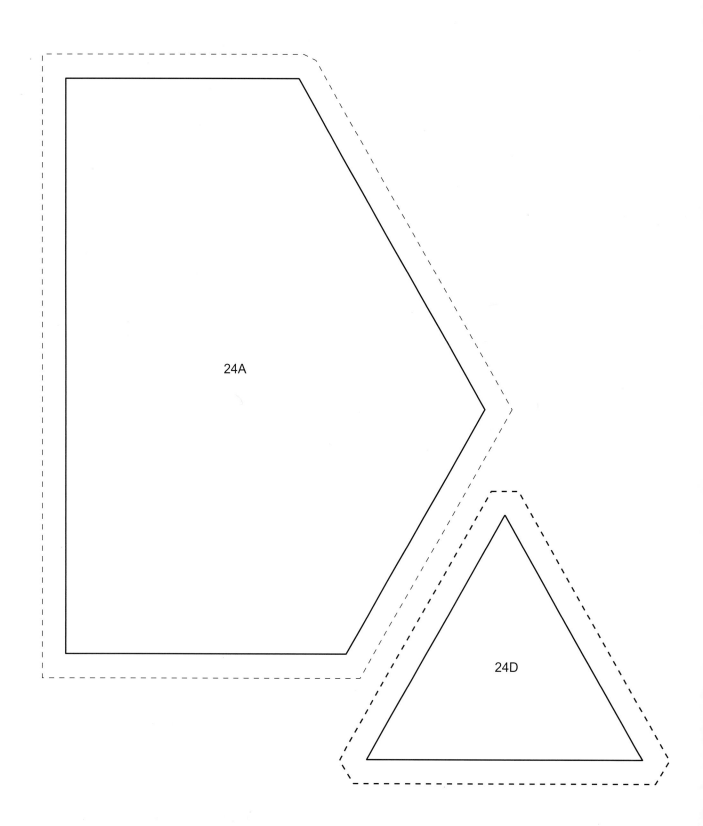

24A

24D

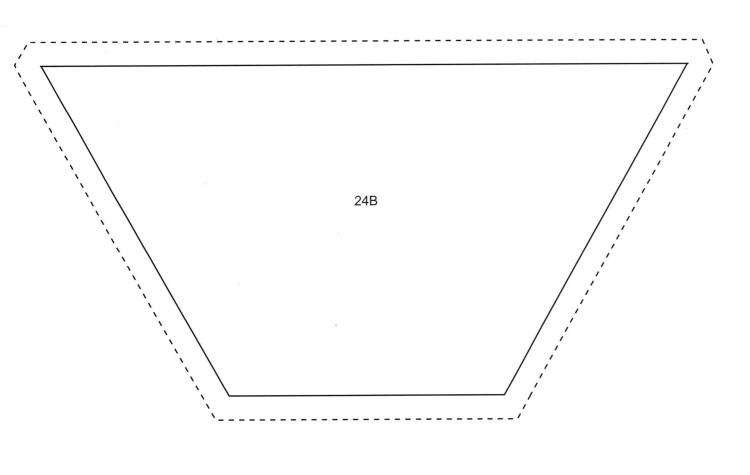

24B

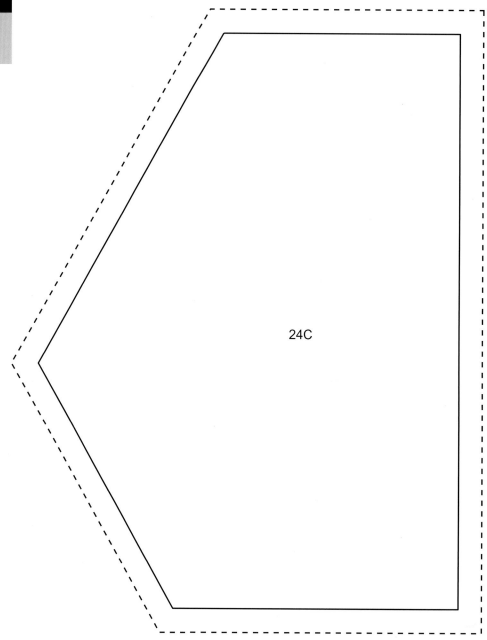

24C

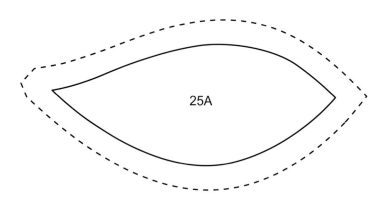

25A

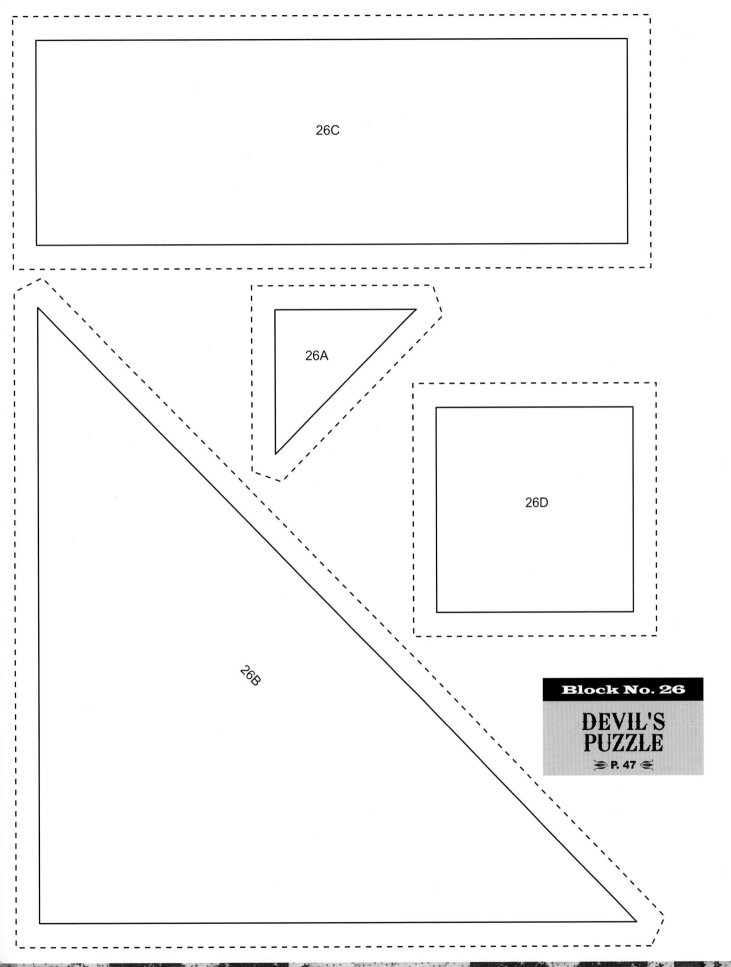

26C

26A

26D

26B

Block No. 26

DEVIL'S PUZZLE

⇒ **P. 47** ⇐

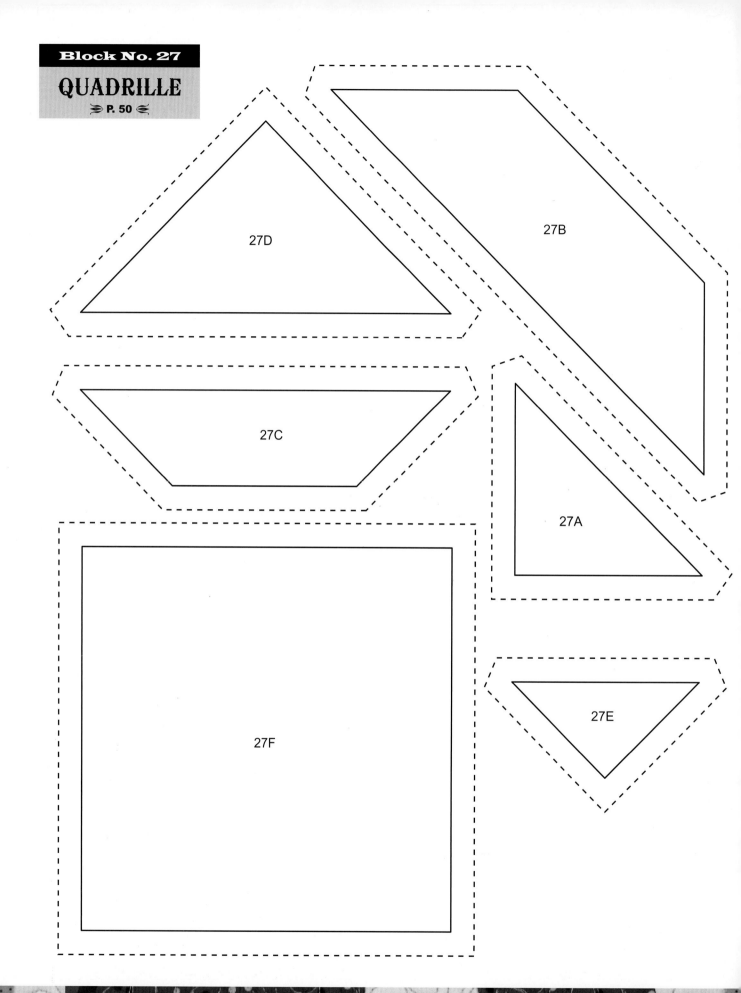

27D

27B

27C

27A

27E

27F

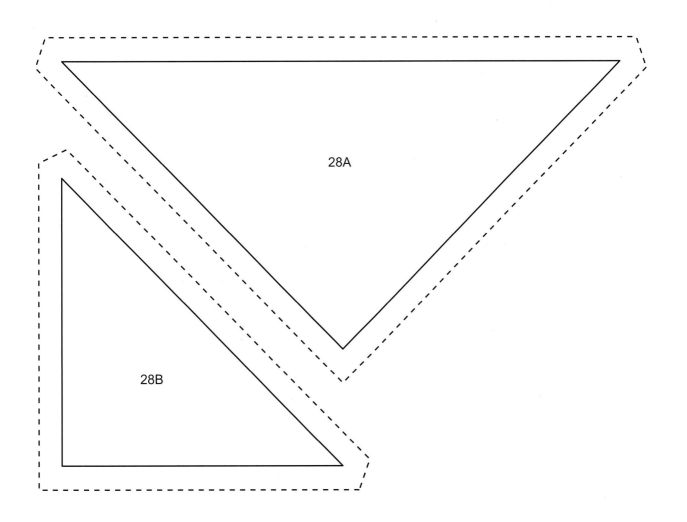

28A

28B

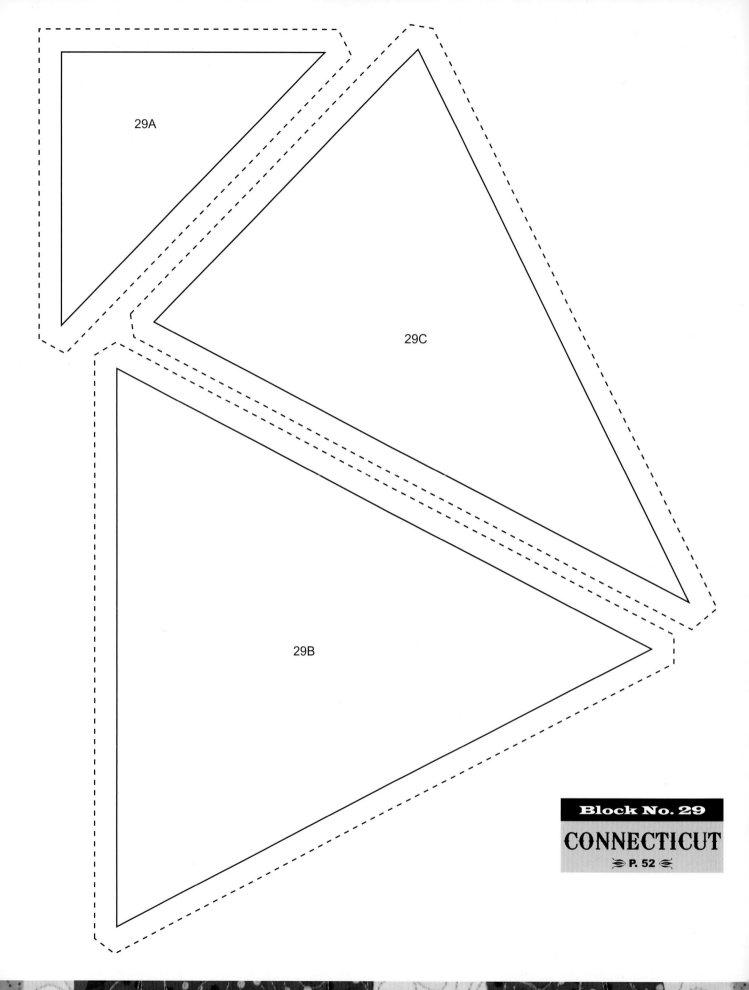

29A

29C

29B

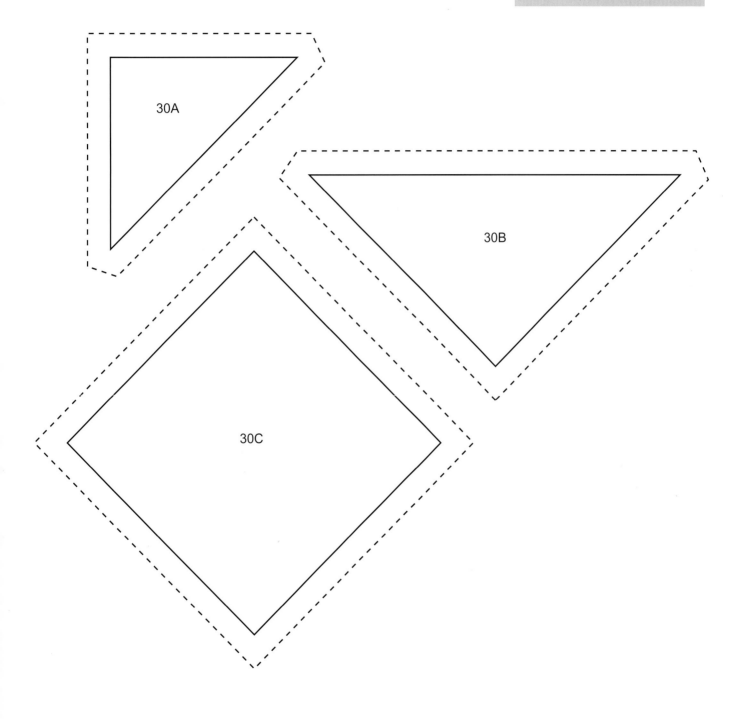

30A

30B

30C

31A

31D

31B

31C

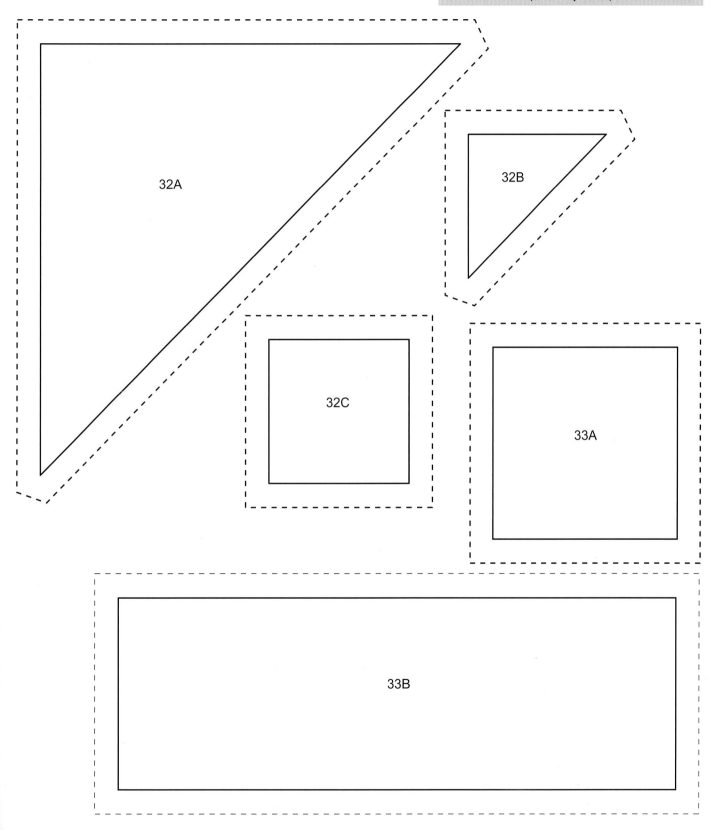

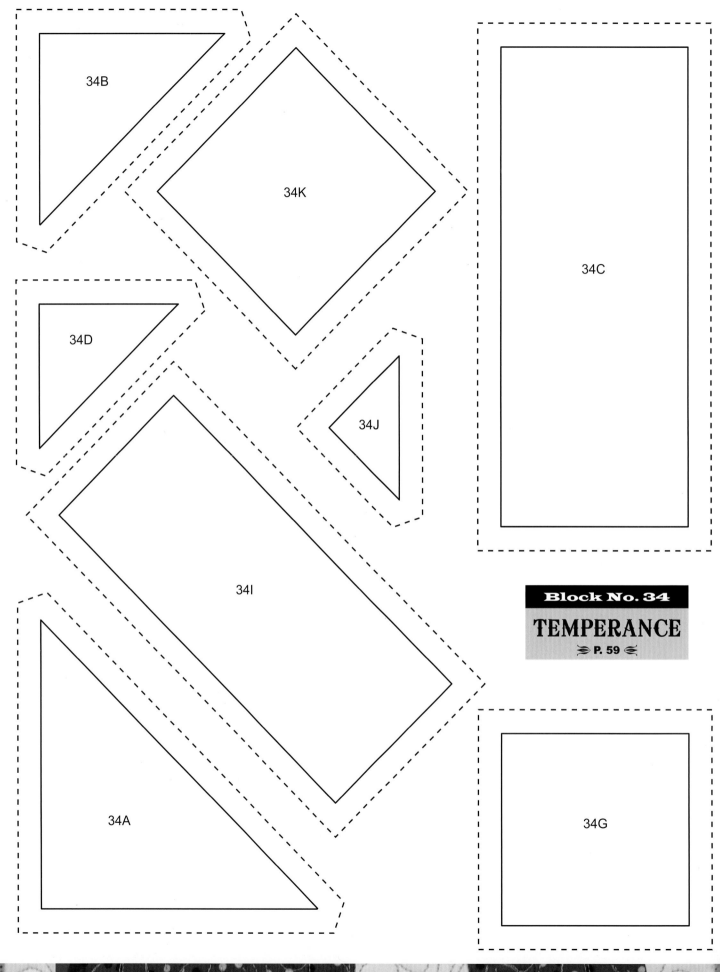

34B

34K

34C

34D

34J

34I

34A

Block No. 34

TEMPERANCE

≽ P. 59 ≼

34G

35A

35C

35D

35E

35B

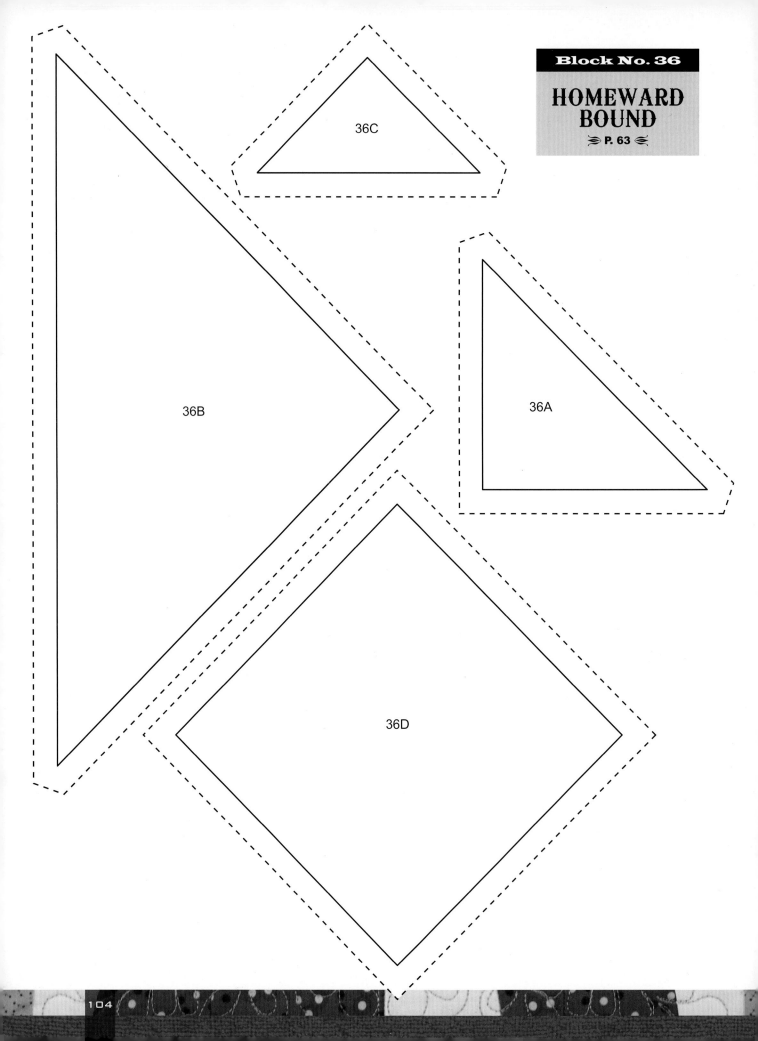

36C

36A

36B

36D

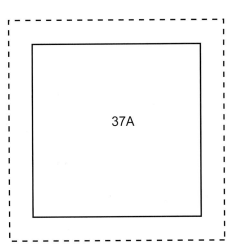

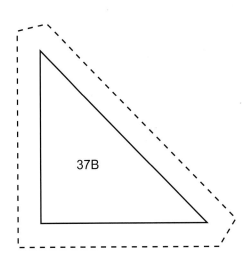

37A

37B

37C

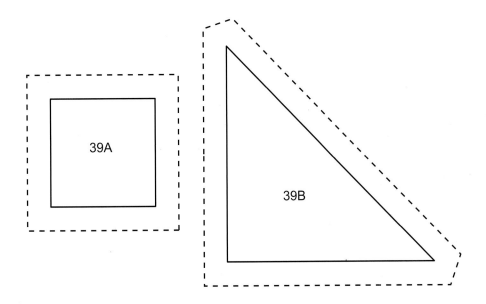

39A

39B

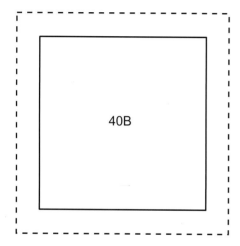

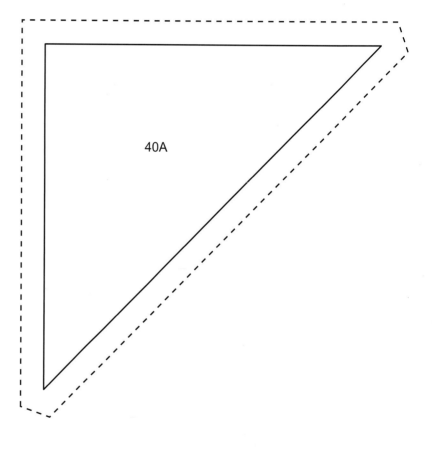

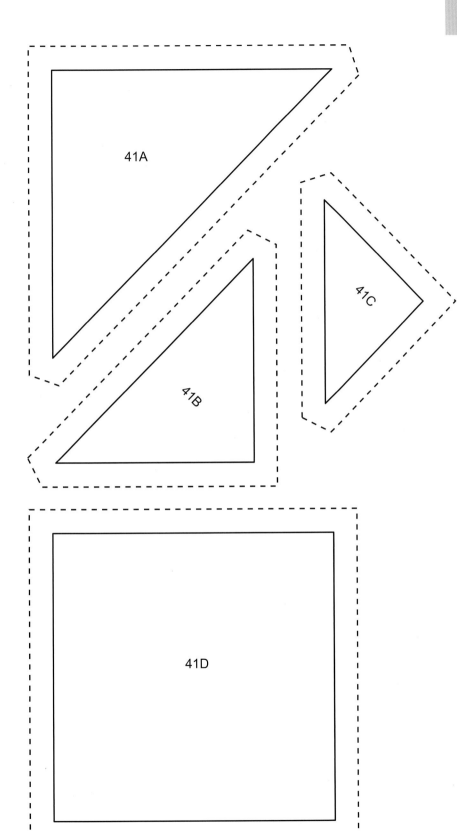

41A

41B

41C

41D

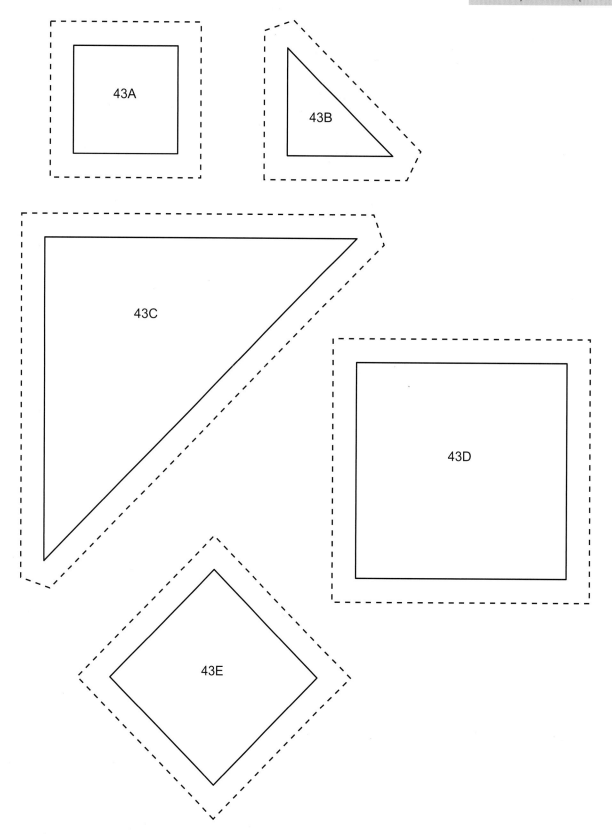

43A

43B

43C

43D

43E

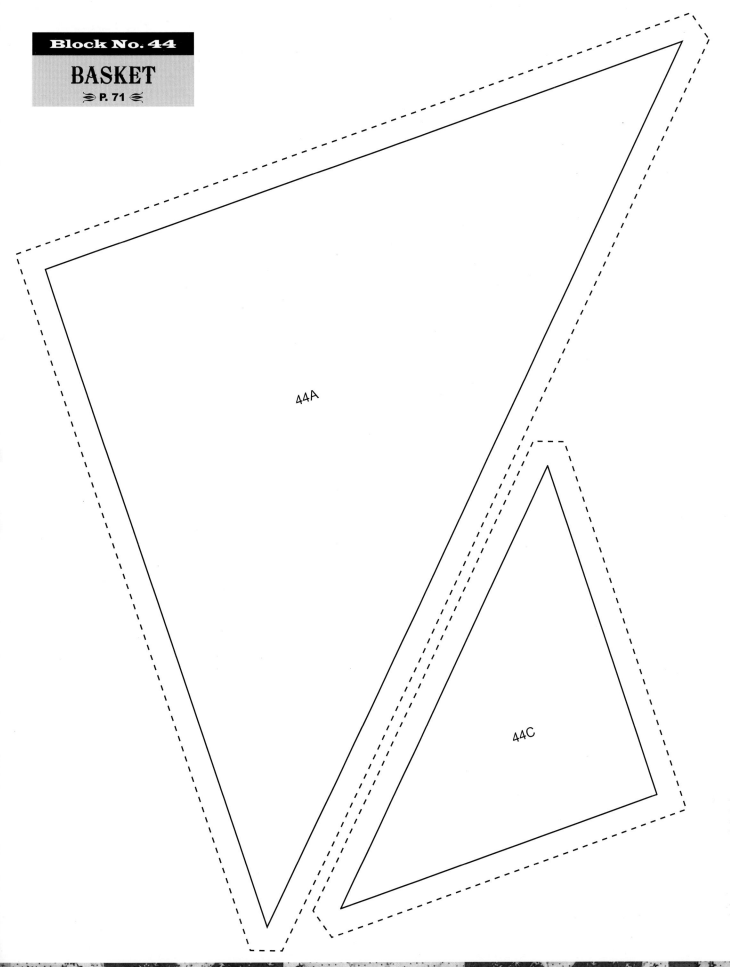

Block No. 44

BASKET

≫ P. 71 ≪

44A

44C

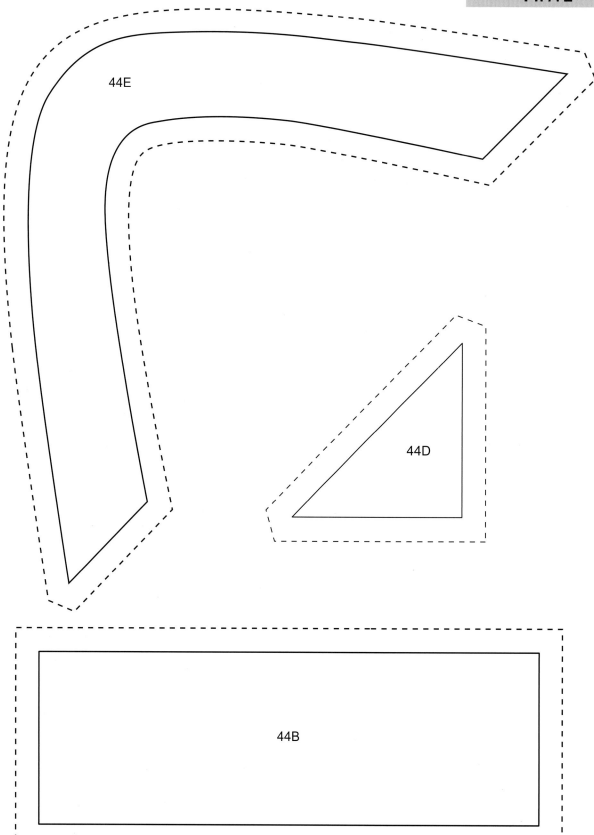

44E

44D

44B

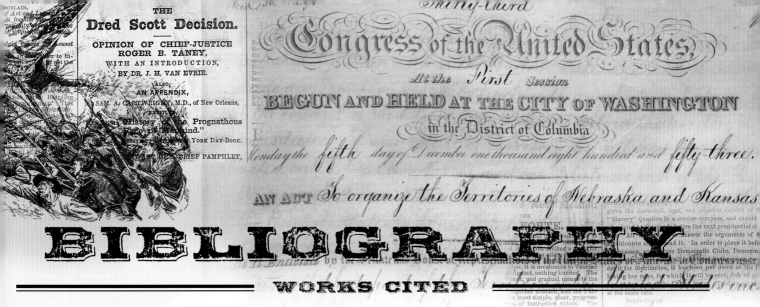

BIBLIOGRAPHY

WORKS CITED

"Abraham Lincoln: Dred Scott Decision." *The History Place*. Web. 09 June 2010. <http://www.historyplace.com/lincoln/dred.htm>.

"Abraham Lincoln: Kansas-Nebraska Act." *The History Place*. 1996. Web. Mar.-Apr. 2010. <http://www.historyplace.com/lincoln/kansas.htm>.

"Africans in America/Part 4/Resource Bank Contents." *PBS*. Web. 09 June 2010. <http://www.pbs.org/wgbh/aia/part4>.

"Dred Scott Case Collection - Chronology." *Washington University Libraries*. Web. 09 June 2010. <http://www.libraries.wustl.edu/vlib/dredscott/chronology.html>.

"Dred Scott." *PBS*. Web. 09 June 2010. <http://www.pbs.org/wgbh.aia/part4/4p2932.html>.

Du, Bois, and John David Smith. *John Brown: a Biography*. Armonk, N.Y.: M.E. Sharpe, 1997. Print.

Finkelman, Paul. *Defending Slavery: Proslavery Thought in the Old South : a Brief History with Documents*. Boston: Bedford/St. Martin's, 2003. Print.

Freehling, William W. *The Road to Disunion*. New York: Oxford UP, 1990. Print.

"Fugitive Slave Act." *United States History*. Web. 09 June 2010. <http://www.u-s-history.com/pages/h137.html>.

Hansen, Harry. *The Civil War: a History*. New York: New American Library, 2002. Print.

"Harpers Ferry." *PBS*. Web. 09 June 2010. <http://www.pbs.org/wgbh/aia/part4/4p2940.html>.

Heidler, David Stephen, Jeanne T. Heidler, and David J. Coles. *Encyclopedia of the American Civil War: a Political, Social, and Military History*. Santa Barbara, Calif.: ABC-CLIO, 2000. Print.

The Impending Crisis 18481861. Paw Prints, 2008. Print.

"John Brown." *PBS*. Web. 09 June 2010. <http://pbs.org/wgbh/aia/part4/4p1550.html>.

"John C. Calhoun." *NNDB: Tracking the Entire World*. Web. 09 June 2010. <http://www.nndb.com/people/902/000043773/>.

"Kansas-Nebraska Act." *United States History*. Web. Mar.-Apr. 2010. <http://www.u-s-history.com/pages/h83.html>.

Kelly, Martin. "Compromise of 1850." *American History From About*. Web. 09 June 2010. <http://americanhistory.about.com/od/beforethewar/g/compromise1850.htm>.

Kelly, Martin. "Lincoln-Douglas Debates - History of the Lincoln-Douglas Debates." *American History From About*. Web. Mar.-Apr. 2010. <http://americanhistory.about.com/od/civilwarmenu/a/lincoln_douglas.htm>.

Life, General Law. "The American Civil War: Quotes - President Abraham Lincoln." *The Battle of Gettysburg & The American Civil War*. Web. 09 June 2010. <http://www.brother-swar.com/Civil_War_Quotes_4c.htm>.

"Lincoln - Douglas Debates of 1858." *Illinois in the Civil War*. Web. Mar.-Apr. 2010. <http://www.illinoiscivilwar.org/debates.html>.

Lincoln, Abraham, and Stephen A. Douglas. *Political Debates between Hon. Abraham Lincoln and Hon. Stephen A. Douglas, in the Celebrated Campaign of 1858 in Illinois: including the Preceding Speeches of Each, at Chicago, Springfield, Etc. : Also the Two Great Speeches of Mr. Lincoln in Ohio, in 1859, as Carefully Prepared by the Reporters of Each Party, and Published at the times of Their Delivery*. Columbus: Follett, Foster and Company, 1860. Print.

"Missouri Compromise — Infoplease.com." *Infoplease: Encyclopedia, Almanac, Atlas, Biographies, Dictionary, Thesaurus. Free Online Reference, Research & Homework Help. — Infoplease.com*. 2005. Web. Mar.-Apr. 2010. <http://www.infoplease.com/ce6/history/A0833427.html>.

19th Century History. Web. Mar.-Apr. 2010. <http://history1800s.about.com/slaveryinamerica/a/kansasnebraska.htm>.

"Nullification — Infoplease.com." *Infoplease: Encyclopedia, Almanac, Atlas, Biographies, Dictionary, Thesaurus. Free Online Reference, Research & Homework Help. — Infoplease. com*. 2005. Web. Apr.-May 2010. <http://www.infoplease.com/ce6/history/A0836166.html>.

Patkus, Ronald D., and Mary C. Schlosser. "Uncle Tom's Cabin: Aspects of the Publishing History." *Home - Archives and Special Collections - Vassar College*. Web. 09 June 2010. <http://specialcollections.vassar.edu/exhibits/stowe/essay2.html>.

"Policies (Rare Book and Special Collections Reading Room, Library of Congress)." *Library of Congress Home*. Web. 09 June 2010. <http://www.loc.gov/rr/rarebook/policies.html>.

"Prints & Photographs Online Catalog." *Library of Congress Home*. Web. 09 June 2010. <http://loc.gov/pictures>.

"Stephen Douglas Quotes." *Famous Quotes and Quotations at BrainyQuote*. Web. 09 June 2010. <http://www.brainyquote.com/quotes/quotes/s/stephendou190130.html>.

"Uncle Tom's Cabin." *Black History Guide and Black History Month*. Web. 09 June 2010. <http://www.africanaonline.com/slavery_toms_cabin.htm>.

Williams, Robert Chadwell. *Horace Greeley: Champion of American Freedom*. New York: New York UP, 2006. Print.

ABOUT THE
AUTHORS

In 2002, Dolores Smith and Sarah Maxwell opened their quilt shop, Homestead Hearth, located in Mexico, Mo. Under that trade name they have since designed quilts that have appeared in most of the major quilting magazines. Their original pattern line debuted in 2009, and is available at their website, **www.homesteadhearth.com** . They also design fabric for Marcus Fabrics. Dolores lives in Mexico with her husband. She has two sons. Sarah also lives in Mexico with her husband and two daughters.

Dolores Smith, left, and Sarah Maxwell are the owners of Homestead Hearth in Mexico, Missouri.

The photographs in this book were taken at the home of Ray and Connie White in Harrisonville, Missouri. Built in 1852 by Abe Cassell, the home has withstood the test of time by adapting and changing. During the Civil War, when Cassell wouldn't pledge his allegiance to the Union, he deeded it to the County Court. In 1867 it served as a schoolhouse, and later it was the schoolhouse for the newly freed slave children.

ABOUT THE
PHOTOGRAPHY

In 1874 the house was purchased by a physician, Thomas Beatie, where he practiced medicine in the front parlor. He reputedly treated both Jesse James and Cole Younger in this room. Throughout the next 100 years it was bought and sold 3 times. The Whites bought it in 1969 and have completely restored it to how it would have been in 1874.